MAGIC

OF NLP

DEMYSTIFIED

A
PRAGMATIC GUIDE
TO
COMMUNICATION
AND CHANGE

Byron A. Lewis
R. Frank Pucelik

Metamorphous Press
Portland, Oregon

Published by

Metamorphous Press
P.O. Box 10616
Portland, OR 97210-0616

Revised Edition: Original copyright under the title "Meta
Principles of Communication and Change: A Model For A
Process Theory of Personality," 1980, Byron A. Lewis.

Copyright © 1990 by Byron Lewis and Frank Pucelik
Cover Design & Editing by Lori Stephens
Illustrations by Leslie Antos
Special thanks to D.C. DuBosque and Lisa Lepine
for assistance on cover design and artwork
Printed in the United States of America

Eighth Printing August 1992

Lewis, Byron A.
Magic of NLP demystified: a pragmatic guide to
communication and change / Byron A. Lewis, R. Frank
Pucelik ; [illustrations by Leslie Antos]. — Rev. ed.
  p. cm.
Rev. ed. of: Magic demystified. Rev. ed. c1982.
Includes bibliographical references.
ISBN 1-55552-017-0
1. Neurolinguistic programming. I. Pucelik, R. Frank.
II. Lewis, Byron A. Magic demystified. III. Title.
158'.1—dc20   90-5742

PREFACE

This work represents the culmination of several years of training and self-exploration within the confines of a specific sphere of study. It was in the early 1970's that I was led through a powerful therapeutic experience by two important people in my life, Frank Pucelik and Leslie Cameron (now Bandler). That session had a profound and lasting effect on me. Soon after the experience I found myself thinking, "I want to learn how to do that kind of magic!" And so I did.

With the help of Leslie and Frank, I became a member of a small experimental-research therapy group in Santa Cruz, California. Thus I became one of a growing number of people who were actually studying the *magic* of therapeutic growth and change. This extremely creative and generative group of people centered around two exciting and charismatic individuals: Richard Bandler and John Grinder. Caught up in the enthusiastic energy of the group, I found my perceptions heightening, my abilities growing, and my own model of the world expanding as if by magic.

It wasn't enough, however, to simply learn how to do this therapeutic wizardry. I wanted to share it with others. I began to compile notebooks detailing my learning experiences and started to see clients under the supervision of therapists who were also interested in the Meta materials. It didn't take long to develop a style of my own, and I labeled my notes "A Model for a Process Theory of Personality." I was sure I had found "The Right Track." It took a while for me to become aware of the trap I had set for myself.

As I read and continued to study and work with people, I discovered that my model was continually being stretched, extended, expanded, and enlarged. But just as often it was also shrunk, crushed, pierced, and mutilated. I was amazed. It was during a moment of quiet desperation that I created a symbolic representation of the wonderful contradictions confronting me. It represents both the confusion I was feeling (don't get me wrong — I thoroughly enjoyed it!) and recognition of the trap from which I was escaping, the trap of thinking that there is only one reliable, accurate, and successful path to therapeutic growth and change. The symbol has held an important place tacked to the wall above my typewriter. It looks like this:

My goal with this book is to present models of basic Meta principles which underlie the "magic" of effective change-oriented communication. However, it is essential to keep in mind how important it is to remain open to experience in order to prevent becoming trapped or limited by a model. Towards that end I have structured parts of this presentation to emphasize that there are always alternatives. We need only learn how to recognize them.

December 27, 1979
Byron A. Lewis

INTRODUCTION

> . . . we must learn to understand the "out-of-awareness" aspects of communication. We must never assume that we are fully aware of what we communicate to someone else. There exists in the world today tremendous distortions in meaning as men try to communicate with one another. (p. 29)
>
> Edward T. Hall
> *The Silent Language*

In his book *Persuasion and Healing*, Jerome Frank identified the major goals of various approaches to psychotherapy. These include efforts to reduce the client's distress, increase his self-esteem, help him to function better at work and in his relationships, and ". . . heighten his sense of control over himself and his environment." (p. 200) It is important to note that, as we become aware of some of those "out-of-awareness" aspects of communication referred to by Hall, we enhance the sense of control that Frank has identified as a major goal of psychotherapy. This book is dedicated to improving our ability to perceive, identify, and utilize certain aspects of the communicative process that are not normally in our conscious awareness.

This is also a book about change. It is a collection of effective tools for assisting in the resolution of problems found in many settings. The patterns discussed can assist anyone to more fully participate in and control the growth experience of positive change.

The Meta principles presented in this book encompass many schools of psychological thought. They include elements from each of the following areas of psychology: *behavioral psychology*, which emphasizes observable behavior and stimulus-response connections; *humanistic psychology*, which stresses free will and subjective experience; *cognitive theory*, which covers the transformation of sensory stimulation in terms of coding, storing in memory, and retrieval systems; *traditional psychotherapy*, which deals with conscious and unconscious distinctions of thoughts, fears, and wishes that may or may not manifest themselves in awareness; and information drawn from various neurological studies, especially studies of changes which occur in the nervous system. The term "meta" is used because the model which is developed is *about* rather than *a part* of all of these, and the emphasis is on the processes of change.

This book does not propose a new approach to psychotherapy, a new "philosophy of life," or a new way to get "IT." What it does offer is the opportunity to experience personality and communication as *processes*. The text presents a blend of research, theory, and relevant portions of transcripts from therapeutic sessions and educational seminars. The emphasis is on models, for it is through them that we can share a wide range of complex experiences. The medium of study is the process of communication, and special attention is paid to areas generally thought to be unconscious or unaware communicative behavior.

It has been my experience that, with the help of a teacher, counselor, or therapist, people are able to resolve many of their problems. There is often a certain degree of change in personality as a result of insight gained or behavioral modifications programmed into the individual during the sessions. This change assists the individual in "coping" with particular difficulties. What these therapeutic experiences usually do not do, however, is systematically create a *reference structure* — a set of experiences — that would enable a person to change his coping patterns in response to *new* difficulties. In my work with people, I have found that by presenting information to them in specific ways, that is, by being explicit about the *processes* involved in change and positive growth, clients can learn to have many of the same resources the teacher and therapist have for solving problems. This systematic *demystification* of normally out-of-awareness aspects of communication gives the client a heightened sense of control over himself and his environment. Although this is not true for every client, the patterns used to obtain the information about a client's communicative behavior remain the same. Various ways of utilizing this information are presented in the text.

Throughout the text, a variety of techniques are provided as pragmatic applications of the material. They also draw the reader's attention to the processes involved in personality development and maintenance. Use of these processes may assist you in helping those you work and live with to discover more choices about how they perceive the world and themselves and what they might do to lead more comfortable and productive lives. The methods covered in this book may be learned quite rapidly. They are not meant, however, to take the place of any currently-in-use psychotherapeutic methodologies. They are offered as an adjunct to existing techniques and as a perceptual paradigm for the serious student of human behavior, communication, and personality.

Throughout this book I interchange the terms "model of the world," "map," and "model of reality." They all stand for the same concept in this book. There are also places where I have shortened the term "representational system" to simply "system." In these cases, the meaning of the word will be obvious from its context.

With some practice, you may soon find many of the techniques and the perceptual acuity presented here coming into use in your everyday patterns of communication, as well as in the professional setting. I invite you to use this book as an opportunity to explore the variables of both internal communication processes and the behavior called communication that we experience continuously as social beings.

ACKNOWLEDGEMENTS

Gratitude is expressed to the following individuals:

To Leslie Cameron-Bandler who showed me the path,

To Richard Bandler who led me down it,

To John Grinder who illuminated it for me, and

To Frank Pucelik who set me back on course (repeatedly) and whose immeasureable input into this volume warranted his co-authorship.

Special thanks go to Ron Hill, Ph.D., Nancy Skolnik, Ph.D., and Linnaea Marvell-Mell, whose editing and helpful suggestions were so instrumental in putting the book into its final form, to Marcia Lewis, my wife, for her support and her illustration on page 117, and to Leslie Antos, my sister, for her beautiful and creative illustrations.

TABLE OF CONTENTS

CHAPTER I

MODELS

The purpose of the model is to enable the user to do a better job in handling the enormous complexities of life. By using models, we see and test how things work and can even predict how things will go in the future. (p. 13)

Edward T. Hall
Beyond Culture

The Use of Models

No other creature we know of is quite as infatuated with the construction and use of models as we humans appear to be. As Hall points out, "We are the model-making organism par excellence." (p. 13) We use these models to represent almost all aspects of our environment, our social organizations, our technology, and even our very life processes. Models of machines, buildings, or bridges help us see and evaluate design and structure. Models of government enable us to understand complex systems of human social behavior. Scientific models assist us in perceiving relationships and properties of theoretical problems and processes.

It is my goal that the psychological and behavioral models presented in this book will operate as Hall suggests. That is, they will reduce the complexities of human communication into a more easily perceived and understandable framework ultimately enabling you to direct yourself and others toward a healthy and positive future.

Neurological Basis

Our romance with constructing models of our experience of the world may have a basis in psychobiological processes. We cannot escape the limitations imposed by our biological origins. As the noted Carl Jung observed:

> Man. . . never perceives anything fully or comprehends anything completely. He can see, hear, touch, taste; but how far he sees, how well he hears, what his touch tells him, and what he tastes depend upon the number and quality of his senses. . . . No matter what instruments he uses, at some point he reaches the edge of certainty beyond which conscious knowledge cannot pass. (p. 21)
>
> *Man and His Symbols*

In our constant attempts to understand, driven by some intrinsic need to explore and explain, we create our models. But we are inexorably separated from the world outside ourselves.[1] Neural transmission, the basis of what we call perception, is a bioelectric phenomenon. Billions of neurons make up the human nervous system. Even though sensory input varies from pressure to temperature to sound to electromagnetic waves, they are all ultimately transformed into electrochemical impulses as they are transmitted to the central nervous system. The study of this miraculous transmutation of energy leads us to a fundamental aspect of experience: we do not perceive *reality*, but rather a neurological *model* of reality. This is what forms the basis for what I call our *model of the world.*

The Nerve Cell

The nerve cell represents the first step in the creation of our models of the world. The basic units of the nerve cell are shown below.

1. *Cell body* containing nucleus.
2. *Dendrites.* These extend from the cell body and form the "receiving area" for stimulation from outside the body and from other adjacent cells.
3. *Axon.* This single fiber transmits the bioelectric impulse to the axon terminal.
4. *Axon terminal.* This is the part of the nerve cell that activates other neurons on the way to or from the central nervous system as well as within it. Neural "messages" are also transmitted to muscles and glands through the axon terminal.

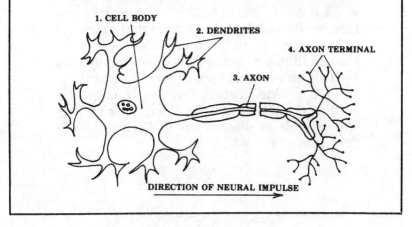

1. CELL BODY
2. DENDRITES
4. AXON TERMINAL
3. AXON
DIRECTION OF NEURAL IMPULSE

Because sensory organs vary greatly from one individual to another, each one of us perceives the world differently. These differences may be subtle or great. But since our perceptions form the basis for our models of the world, we must assume that every individual will have a *different* model.

The Reality Model

Due to similarities in neurological mechanisms in each of us, we are able to have similar experiences. These, combined with shared social and cultural experiences, enable the creation of what might be called "consensus realities." These are shared models that form the basis of our social structures. Language is the prime example of such a model. However, it is the fact that there can be no universally shared and accepted representation of experience, no one model of the world that is accurate for everyone, that accounts for the marvelous diversity found in the human personality.

Perceptions Can Be Deceiving

There is an interesting exhibit at the "Exploratorium" in San Francisco. Two half-inch copper tubes are wound side-by-side around a wooden dowel. Warm fluid is piped through one tube, while cold fluid flows through the other. It is quite a shock to touch or grasp the bundle: the simultaneous sensations of warm and cold produce an extremely hot or burning sensation. It is fun to watch disbelieving people jump after reading the description and then, thinking they will be able to discern the difference, take a firm grasp of the bundle!

HOT WATER

COLD WATER

Patterns of Rule-Governed Behavior

Although it is important to appreciate the individual nature of perceived reality, it is equally important to identify *patterns* of behavior exhibited by individuals and groups. The observation of these patterns forms the central theme of this work. In his book, *The Silent Language,* E.T. Hall states that, "The goal of the investigator who deals with human phenomena is to discover the patterns. . . that exist hidden in the minds, the sensory apparatus, and the muscles of man." (p. 115) These bits and pieces of observable behavior go into the making of the process-oriented model of personality presented in this book.

During interactions involved in communication, certain consistencies of behavior become evident. Just as the language we use is structured by semantics and grammar, so does the rich and varied nonlinguistic behavior of humans appear to follow a highly structured order. We are, however, confronted with the same dilemma that has long faced linguists. The native speaker of any language forms his speech without any necessary awareness of the rules being used. Likewise, the rules of nonlinguistic behavior are veiled by their very nature: they are *unconscious processes.* In both cases we must study these rules by analyzing their end products: language and behavior. As Watzlawick, Beavin, and Jackson stated in *Pragmatics of Human Communication*, the goal comes down to observing these processes exhibited through language and behavior in an attempt to identify a "complex pattern of redundancies." (p. 37) A good enough model, says Watzlawick, will give us the ability to evaluate, predict, and influence behavior.

In *The Structure of Magic, Volume I,* Richard Bandler and John Grinder introduce a set of elegant tools for organizing and describing our observations. There are three mechanisms common to all model-building activities: *generalization, deletion,* and *distortion.* Bandler and Grinder call these the "universal human modeling processes."[2] These three processes operate at every stage in the construction and use of our models of the world. They underlie our abilities to concentrate, to plan and learn, and to dream. They become evident to the trained observer through a person's speech and behavior, and learning to detect and utilize these universal processes is a central theme of this book.

Generalization

The process of generalization provides part of the explanation of how we are able to learn as rapidly as we do. Many "new" behaviors, for example, are actually composed of bits and pieces of previously experienced behaviors which are similar to the new behavior. Because of this similarity, we are able to generalize from the experience of the old behavior, alleviating the need to learn the new behavior "from scratch." The ability to generalize from past experiences means that it is not necessary to expend great amounts of time and energy learning new behaviors. This same process is utilized in the learning of new concepts and in other activities associated with what we call "thinking." In essence, generalization eliminates the necessity to relearn a concept or behavior every time we are confronted with a variation of the original.

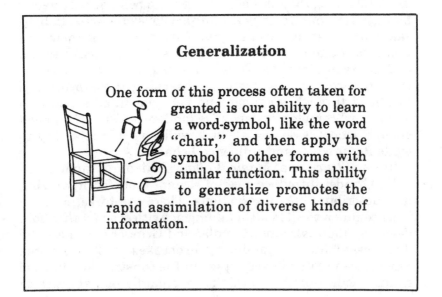

Generalization

One form of this process often taken for granted is our ability to learn a word-symbol, like the word "chair," and then apply the symbol to other forms with similar function. This ability to generalize promotes the rapid assimilation of diverse kinds of information.

Deletion

It has been reported that the human central nervous system is being fed more than two million pieces of information *every second*. Just in terms of efficiency, if every bit of this information had to be processed and used, the time and energy necessary would be astronomical! This is where the process of deletion comes in. Our central nervous system actually operates as a "screening mechanism" enabling us to function at peak efficiency. As Aldous Huxley says in *The Doors of Perception*, experience "has to be funneled through the reducing valve of the brain and nervous system. What comes out the other end is a measly trickle of the kind of consciousness which will help us to stay alive on the surface of this particular planet." (p. 23)

Obviously, our ability to delete portions of the barrage of input is essential to our survival.

Deletion

Paris in the
the spring.

A snake in the
the grass.

A kick in the
the rear.

One of my favorite examples of deletion is portrayed in the above three sentences. In order to make sense of what you see, there is a tendency to delete the portion of the sentence that doesn't make sense. Notice the extra "the" in each of the sentences. Many people do not even see it when it is pointed out to them. As we shall see, this process has some profound implications in the area of human communication.

8

Distortion

The third universal human modeling process forms the basis for most acts of creativity. Distortion is the process by which we alter our perceptions, changing our experience of sensory input. Using this process we both create and enjoy works of art, music and literature. It also makes possible our ability to dream, fantasize, and plan for the future. By allowing us to manipulate our perceptions of reality, of the word as we *sense* it or *remember* it to be, distortion enables us to create totally unique variables. Some of our "creations" may even be outside the realm of possibility defined by our model of reality. But whether it results in a "quantum leap" in our thinking or simply enables us to "interpret" a Picasso, distortion is an important process in our modeling of the world.

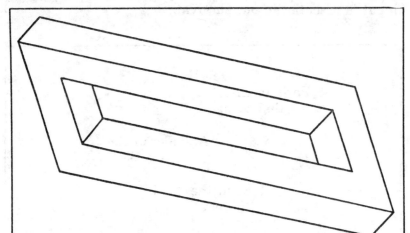

The figure above represents a "visual paradox." Because it presents conflicting information, the observer finds himself attempting to make sense of an apparent irrational figure. This *distortion* occurs because of the capacity of the brain to take in certain kinds of information, in this case a two-dimensional set of lines, and transform it into something that is non-existent: a three-dimensional form.

These remarkable model-building processes of generalization, deletion, and distortion, however, are double-edged. As important as they are to our abilities to learn, think, and create, these same processes can also create pain and suffering in an individual. How do these indispensable tools create pain? How do they limit perception and disallow behavior? How do they become counter-productive to a person's normal living and growing? They do these things by performing their functions just as they are designed. The following examples will demonstrate how these processes can work both for and against the best interests of an individual.

Case Study

Several years ago, I had a client who demonstrated perfectly the duality in function of the universal human modeling processes. What follows are highlights from some of our sessions that exemplify these processes in action.

As a child, Sharon had several very pleasant experiences in a particular reading group. These experiences were soon generalized to *all* reading, and Sharon became an enthusiastic "bookworm." This can be considered a positive example of the process of generalization.

One of the reasons Sharon decided to come in for counseling was what she termed "a fear of men." This "fear" kept her from relaxing enough to have any close, affectionate relationships. In her words, "Men frighten me. I'm afraid all they want is to take advantage of me." We quickly uncovered where her fear had come from: Sharon recounted a severely traumatic experience she had had with a man when she was a young teenager. From this one terrible experience she had begun to generalize about the "motives" of men. These generalizations had become a part of her model of the world and effectively prevented her from enjoying the close, loving relationship that she so dearly wanted. As with her experiences with reading, this modeling process occurred "automatically," completely out of her conscious awareness.

Assumptions Are Generalizations

Some folks I know did an experiment with their bathroom door. Taking the doorknob from a regular door, they mounted it on a nonlatching, one-way swinging door. To open their bathroom door, all you had to do was push on it; it would swing closed automatically. The trick was that they placed the "fake" doorknob on the same side of the door as the hinges. The results of the experiment proved interesting.

Children, they said, generally had no problem discovering the "trick" and were able to get into the bathroom. However, when adults tried the doorknob and found that the door wouldn't open, they *assumed* that it was either stuck or locked. Their assumption, of course, was based on generalizations from past experiences with locked and stuck doors. This part of their models of the world did not allow for the exploration necessary to discover the trick, and they consistently failed to gain entry without the "help" of their hosts.

One of the ways that Sharon was able to be such a good reader was her ability to keep noises and external visual stimuli from distracting her. She had learned to systematically delete from her awareness anything that would detract from her ability to concentrate on the book she was reading. This can be a very productive utilization of the process of deletion.

In the years following her traumatic encounter, Sharon also systematically deleted from her awareness the positive, normal responses of men who became genuinely interested in her. Her "selective attention" only allowed her to be aware of the things they did to "take advantage" of her. Because her model of the world did not include the possibility of warm, kind, and honest attention between men and women, she was not aware of these qualities when they were present in a male admirer. Without this awareness, no healthy relationship could develop.

Again, operating without conscious awareness, deletion can assist us by focusing our attention when necessary, as in the example of Sharon's reading. However, the same process can often be the major source of a person's emotional distress. It can create limitations on our models of the world that prevent us from being able to perceive what we need in order to achieve our goals.

Selective Attention Is Deletion

Sharon loved to read novels. By creatively employing the process of distortion, she could transform words into full, rich experiences. She actually "lived" characters as she read about them. She felt their joys and sorrows, labored in the muddy fields and had tea with the Queen. As a youngster, Sharon had learned to read words and then to distort them into images, feelings, sounds, tastes, and smells so vividly that they became "real" to her. She could talk about different times and far-away places as if she had actually been there. And she could equally well "project" herself into a history book or encyclopedia. This talent played an important part in her choice of careers as a writer and lecturer.

Sharon also used the process of distortion as a means for explaining her "predicament" with men. Though her fear was a major factor, she attributed much of the problem to a series of "bad relationships." As she said, "If only those relationships had been different, if only they had given me what I wanted and needed, then I probably would be a lot happier now." Using the same process that she used to *place herself into* the characters she read about, Sharon indicated by those words that she had effectively *removed herself from* the external world during specific periods in her life.

In her model of the world, it was "relationships" which caused her problems. However, this indicates a distortion of her perception of the situation. A relationship is a *process* involving active participation.[3] By saying that "the relationships" hadn't given her what she wanted, she was ignoring her own reponsibility and participation in the process of relating. She had *removed* herself from the role of participant and had become a helpless observer. This distortion, built into her model of the world, effectively prevented her from being able to change in ways which would make her more comfortable and happy. Not until she could *step back* into the process of relating would she be able to make those changes and regain a sense of control over her own life.

Fantasy is Distortion

The construction of our models of the world may be what James Coleman[4] is referring to when he says that an individual builds a "frame of reference" or "a set of assumptions concerning fact, possibility, and value." He describes how this "inner cognitive map" determines how a person will perceive reality and how he will behave. Of importance here is what happens when a person's map or model has built-in errors. As he says, "... faulty assumptions have important implications for adjustive behavior." A person who follows this erroneous map "... may bristle at nonexistent bogeymen and be unaware of real hazards. To the extent that his view is distorted, he will adjust to a world that does not exist, and will inevitably make miscalculations that will lead to failure and self devaluation." (p. 167)

Trust: Gaining Rapport

Who can deny that the important vector in any type of psychotherapeutic relationship is the establishment of good rapport? (p. 19)
W. S. Korger and
W.D. Fezler: *Hypnosis and Behavior Modification*

In his book *Persuasion and Healing*, Jerome Frank isolates some of the variables that make up a successful therapeutic relationship, especially aspects of the relationship that result in the patient's "susceptibility to the therapist's influence." (p. 197) Of particular interest here is the emphasis put on several variables: the client's expectations and his trust in the therapist, and what he calls "personal attributes of the therapist." Frank found that these factors greatly influence the outcome of therapy.

A study conducted by Strupp, et al.,[5] singled out the patient's trust in the therapist as a singularly important variable. As they stated, "This faith in the integrity of the therapist as a person may be called the capstone of a successful therapeutic relationship subsuming other characteristics." (p. 36)

In any close or intimate relationship, trust becomes a primary element. This section will begin to explore the various ways this trust develops and the effects it has on the rapport so essential to an effective relationship.

As previously mentioned, Jerome Frank noted that particular attributes of the therapist himself are important ingredients of the therapeutic relationship. From questionnaires filled out by their patients, Frank found these attributes to include the therapist's ability to be a "... keenly interested. . . concerned listener. . .who speaks one's language [and] makes sense. . . ." (p. 185) The development of trust, then, may begin when a person gets the sense that he is being understood, that he and the other person are "speaking the same language." Think for a moment about the people in your life whom you consider to be *influential*. This ability to influence you and others is based in large part on the trust given them by those who believe they are "understanding." Of course, this is an oversimplification. However, especially in the therapeutic setting, this trust is often a necessary condition for a successful therapeutic relationship. Trust must also exist between friends, or the relationship falters. A business deal cannot be consummated unless there is a mutual trust based on the belief that each party is being understood by the other.

What is it about particularly influential individuals that

leads to this trust? What observable behaviors do these wizards of communication exhibit that we might identify and use ourselves in our own professional and personal relationships? As these questions are answered, you will begin to discover some of the practical strategies for creating positive change.

Being Understood

One of the most important ingredients in being influential is the ability to elicit the belief that you understand. Understanding implies that you can "join" a person at his own model of the world. This is important because people tend to operate as if their model of the world *is* the *real* world. Understanding is the crucial bridge between our model of the world and theirs.

Logical Typing Errors

Gregory Bateson illustrates the distinction between "reality" and our models of reality with a menu card analogy.[6] We tend to operate on the assumption that a "thing" and its "name" are one and the same. Bateson calls this a "logical typing error." It is like walking into a restaurant, says Bateson, and being handed a menu card. Since the menu merely represents the food, we might consider it to be a map or model of reality. However, if we treat

the menu like we often treat our own models of the world — as if it actually *is* reality — we would begin to eat the menu! As Bateson points out, "Expectably, communicating organisms... will mistake map for territory. . . ." (p. 402)

To take the metaphor a step further, sometimes we are surprised by the food we have ordered from the menu. When it arrives, we may not even like it, though we liked what was represented by the menu. Ideally, we would be able to go into a restaurant, stop by the kitchen, and sample the food before we decided. Even then, however, we couldn't be absolutely sure of what we would get when the waiter brought our food. But at least we might have a better idea.

We cannot actually "sample" reality as the metaphor suggests. All we ever have are menus: models of reality which we tend to believe *are* what they merely *represent.*

There are several ways you can "join" a person at his own model of the world. These will be covered in following sections and chapters. As you acknowledge an individual's model of the world by joining him with your language and with other behaviors that let him know that you understand, you pave the way for highly effective and influential communication to occur. This does not mean that you accept his model as your own, but rather that you instill the trust and rapport so important in close or intimate relationships and create the ideal climate for positive growth and change.

Constraints on the Model

For every organism there are limitations and regularities which define what will be learned and under what circumstances this learning will occur. (p. 416)

Gregory Bateson
Steps to an Ecology of Mind

The construction of our models of the world is not a haphazard, disorganized process. It is a highly efficient, ongoing procedure that operates throughout our whole lifetime. The "information" used in the construction of our models, the experiences and memories of experiences that form the building blocks of the structure, are forced through certain constraints or "filters" on the model-building process. There are three constraints or filters which have been identified by Bandler and Grinder.[7] These are *neurological, social,* and *individual* constraints. Knowing the ways that these filters affect our models of the world can assist us in better observing the behavioral patterns that will enable us to both predict and influence with remarkable success the behavior of our clients, students, and others with whom we communicate.

Neurological Constraints

It is through our neurological makeup, our sense organs and nerves, that we initially receive information about the world. However, due to individual differences and the fact that "raw" information is translated into bioelectric impulses, we are inexorably separated from the "real world." Our neurology filters the experience, and, because everyone's "filters" are slightly different, we can assume that everyone's model of the world will be different. This phenomenon underlies the idea that we do not react to the "real world" but rather on our own personal model of the world.

The Study of Perception

A term common to the study of perception is *absolute threshold*. This is the minimum amount of physical energy necessary to stimulate a sense organ into firing off a signal to the central nervous system (CNS). This means that there are potential sensory signals from our environment that are never even "received" or sensed. Our sensory organs not only channel information into our CNS but also effectively filter it as it comes in. For example, we know that there are sounds both above and below the ability of the human ear to hear, and we know that there are non-visible areas of the electro-magnetic spectrum. This knowledge has been gained through the use of artificial mechan-isms which translate or re-present these areas into perceivable stimuli. A good portion of my work as a teacher and counselor is to operate much like those machines. That is, I work to re-present aspects of the environment that they are filtering out or deleting from their experi-ence. There will be more on that in upcoming sections.

Difference threshold is another term used in the study of perception. This is the minimum amount of stimulation necessary to be able to detect a difference between two similar stimuli. This just noticeable difference (j.n.d.) supports the notion that our receptor organs act as filters to our perception of the world.

Another important concept in the study of perception is the fact that our sensory mechan-isms operate on a process called *recurrent inhibition*. Because of this neural mechanism, we tend to receive information from our senses primarily about *changes* in our environment rather than about constant or unchanging aspects of experience. One of the reasons for including a good bottle of wine with a meal is to stimulate our gustatory-olfactory sensing organs between bites of food. The wine literally changes the environment in our mouths so that each bite will taste just as savory as the first.

Recurrent inhibition is what underlies the tendency to cease paying attention to static, unchanging aspects of our environment. It is interesting to speculate about how this neuro-logical mechanism might affect our experience of the world on a broader scale. Noam Chom-

sky (see Chapter III), quoting Viktor Shklov-
skij, writes:

"People living at the seashore grow so
accustomed to the murmur of the waves
that they never hear it. By the same
token, we scarcely ever hear the words
which we utter.... We look at each other,
but we do not see each other any more.
Our perception of the world has withered
away; what has remained is mere recognition." (p. 24-25)

Our sensory systems provide us with very pleasant
experiences in many ways. Movies, which are actually only
rapidly flashed "still" pictures, give us the illusion of motion.
We can also experience strong emotional feelings while
sitting in a theater watching and listening to a film. It is
important to understand that these same abilities, these
neurological processes which enable us to have pleasant
experiences, also operate at times to give us pain by *limiting*
our perceptions and our ability to adequately respond to our
environment.

As the discussion of these processes continues, I hope to
demonstrate that there are consistencies in how people
experience the world and how they create their models of
what they experience. These consistencies can assist us in
more effectively communicating with them. By enabling us
to predict and influence behavior, observing and utilizing
these consistencies can help us assist the people we live and
work with in making different choices about how to feel and
how to respond, choices which will enhance a positive and
enriched perception of the world.

Figure 1 - 1 shows the first step in the formulation of our
models of the world. Raw experience is filtered through our
sensory organs (neurological constraints). The experience is
"transformed" into a neurological model including four basic
parameters: vision, feeling, sound, and smell and taste.
Following the model proposed by Bandler and Grinder,[8]
these are labeled, respectively, *V* for vision, *K* for feelings, *A*

for sounds, and *OG* for smell and taste. For every moment there is one complete "set" of these experiences. Each of these sets is called a *4-tuple*.

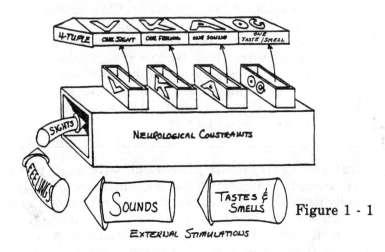

Figure 1 - 1

Social Constraints

Another way we create differences in our models is through social constraints. This filter might be thought of as the second level in the model-building process, coming just after neurological constraints. The primary example of social constraints is *language*, which operates on our models of the world in two primary and apparently opposite ways. One way is to *enhance* and the other is to *limit* our perception of the world around us. It does this by encoding perceptual phenomena into labels (words) which are manipulated by the mind in its efforts to make sense out of experience.[9] For example, Eskimos have some seventy different words for *snow*.[10] They are able to make distinctions about the quality and structure of snow that are beyond the abilities of most individuals in the rest of the world. Obviously this has great survival value to the Eskimo culture. This deeply rooted social constraint, exhibited in the Eskimo language, expands their models of the world to include perceptions that people from other linguistic backgrounds are unable to observe.

An interesting phenomenon occurs when someone becomes fluent in a language different from his native tongue.

As J. Samuel Bois, the general semanticist, observes in *The Art of Awareness,* ". . .I don't see the same things, don't observe the same events, when I change from my French to my English brain." He goes on to say, "Changing my language changes me as an observer. It changes my world at the same time." (p. 20)

Figure 1 - 2 shows the language component being added to the 4-tuple. This either accentuates certain aspects of the neurological model or deletes or distorts it. It can enhance perception as in the case of the Eskimos. Even though I could stand side-by-side with an Eskimo and look at the snow, we would not "see" the same thing because our models of the world are different. The same is true of individuals who come into therapy. As we shall see, it is often through their language that their limited or distorted perception of the world can be known. With this knowledge we can assist them in learning new ways to *talk about* their experiences, ways that will ultimately change their models of the world.

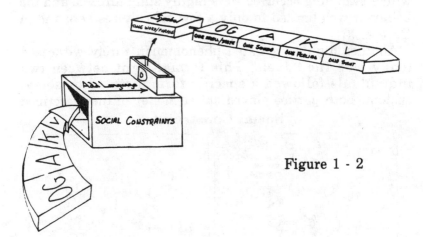

Figure 1 - 2

There are other forms of social constraints that affect a person's modeling process. As Coleman[11] put it, ". . . his personality development reflects both the larger society in which he lives — its institutions, traditions, values, ideas, and technologies — and the immediate family and other interpersonal relationships. . . ." (p. 78) Social customs and conventions are learned and integrated by an individual in much the same ways language is learned. By watching and listening to others and by being corrected when we "error," we come to know what is expected by social convention. Like language, these social rules vary from generation to generation and between the subcultures that make up the larger society. Much like rules that govern language, these social constraints are powerful filters on our models of the world, affecting both perception and behavior. As the following examples will demonstrate, social constraints form some of the boundaries between what we believe to be possible and impossible, good and bad, appropriate and inappropriate, etc.

In the recent past, both in this country and in parts of Western Europe, it was customary for a woman to faint or "swoon" in certain situations. In movies from that period, there was always someone in the crowd ready with smelling salts to help revive the distressed maiden. The situations in which swooning occurred were highly standardized, and the behavior was limited to only a few subcultures here and in Europe.

Another highly regulated phenomenon rarely witnessed today was the "duel." This formal fight between two individuals followed a specific form dictated by social custom. Both parties played out each step of the prescribed

Social Constraints

sequence of responses. The form was rigid and predictable, and everyone knew what was expected.

A more current example of social constraints concerns socially imposed "rules" governing direct eye contact.[12] There are subcultures in the United States that believe that if one man stares directly into the eyes of another man, it is a "challenge," much like the traditional "glove-in-the-face slap" that initiated the duel ritual. In these situations, again highly regulated by custom, there are specific things that each man is expected to do. The challenge is either accepted or declined, depending on the response of the second man to the initiating stare.

Problems may result if two or more individuals are combined from different subcultures with different rules or customs. In an institutional setting, for example, where many differing subcultures are forced to co-mingle, inability to predict expected responses creates the potential for very volatile interactions. For those responsible for maintaining order, the process of "keeping the peace" becomes a labrious and sometimes harrowing experience.

Any time we are confronted with a situation where two models differ, as in the above example, it becomes crucial to determine what the *rules* are for each of the models. These social constraints on the models, properly utilized, are invaluable in the process of gaining rapport, in "speaking the same language" of the parties involved. Using these rules can help create the trust and free-flowing communication necessary for successful positive interventions. Understanding the impact of social constraints on the communication process is one of the ways of orienting yourself to the inevitable differences in each individual's model of the world. Identifying and then honoring these constraints will prevent them from blocking the communication process.

Individual Constraints

As pointed out by L.R. Ferguson in *Personality Development*, "'Personality' is a term that has been defined more variously than perhaps any other general concept in psychology." (p. 2) Taking into account an individual's genetic makeup, Ferguson makes a valid argument for an interpretation of personality based on a knowledge of that individual's *personal history*. Individual constraints, the third in the series discussed here, are the direct result of personal experiences. Taken as a whole, they are what form a person's historical background.

Individual constraints are based on both neurological and social constraints, the two underlying filters of experience. As a person continues the process of construction and modification of his model of the world, it is individual constraints that form the fabric of his belief and value systems. They play an important part in what makes up the "rose" in a person's "rose-colored glasses." It is personal history in part that explains why a ghetto youth is less likely to score as high on the Stanford-Binet intelligence test as a youngster from an "upper class" family. These constraints also account for part of the diversity of scores on tests like the Minnesota Multiphasic Personality Inventory.

Important to our understanding of individual models of the world is the concept of *internally generated stimuli*. As previously mentioned, for every moment in time, we create a 4-tuple of experience. This includes the parameters of visual experience (V); feelings, which include tactile, proprioceptive, and somatic experiences (K); the experience of sound (A); and smell and taste, also known as olfactory and gustatory experience (OG). We also have an immense collection of stored experiences, called memories. These memories can be manipulated, shuffled, and reorganized in very creative ways, something we generally call "thinking." Thinking, however, is merely *synthetic experience*, extrapolations and recombinations of previously experienced material in new and unique ways.

It is possible at any time to substitute synthesized elements for other sensory-based experiences in a 4-tuple. In other words, at any given moment, a person may experience combinations of internally-generated pictures, images, feelings, sounds, smells and tastes along with stimuli of external origin. The smell of a Christmas tree, for example, may originate in the external environment. However, it may instantaneously elicit internally generated visual memories, feelings, and sounds associated with that particular smell.

These synthesized elements in the 4-tuple are based on a person's previous experiences his past personal history, in combination with various wants and needs of the moment. Synthetic experiences are also subject to the universal modeling processes of generalization, deletion, and distortion.

Internal Experience

"Emotionally-laden" experiences are often elicited by cues in the external environment. They may be pleasant, as in the above example, or they may be devastating. An example of internally generated dysfunctional response to external cues is given on page 123.

Figure 1 — 3 show the 4-tuple going through the Individual filter. It is at this point in the formation of the experience the perception of "one moment in time", that a person adds synthesized elements to the 4-tuple. The model shows these internally generated experiences riding "piggyback" on the 4-tuple. For each element in a 4-tuple, a person is only *aware* of one aspect, either the internal or the external experience, but not both at the same time. It is also important to note that although there will always be input from the external environment (except in cases of neurological damage, such as blindness), there does not necessarily have to be an associated internally generated experience for each element in the 4-tuple. For simplicity, the model below shows a complete set of synthesized experiences riding atop the external 4-tuple.

As we shall see in later chapters, people can systematically delete one particular element from their 4-tuples. The ability of a therapist to detect and utilize this kind of information when working with an individual can greatly expedite the process of therapeutic growth and change. The example on page 123 demonstrates how this information can be effectively used.

As the figure shows, the 4-tuples are finally collected in the *Memory Box*. The repository for all experiences, it represents our personal history, our composite model of the world. This collection of experiences does much to shape our thinking and our perception of the world around us. Information for synthetic experiences in this simplistic diagram comes from the Memory Box through the *Memory Tube*. Again, this information can be in the form of a complete internally generated 4-tuple, or it can be single elements from the various stored 4-tuples which "replace" one or more of the pieces of external origins.

A complete diagram showing all three processes is presented in Appendix A.

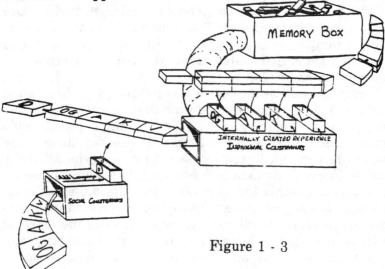

Figure 1 - 3

When we communicate with people, when we are success-ful in creating therapeutic changes, or in teaching something new, we always begin at the neurological level with the sound of our voices and the look and feel of our actions. When intervention ocurs at the linguistic level (see Chapter III), we are operating on a person's 4-tuple at the level of social constraints. At the level of individual constraints, we assist people in understanding how their models of the world are dysfunctional, how they are causing unnecessary pain and hardship in their lives, or how they block the awareness of alternative thoughts, feelings or actions.

Ultimately, any learning or therapeutic experience that is successful becomes a part of a person's personal history. Filed into his *Memory Box,* the new model will begin to shape thinking and perception in new, positive, and healthy ways.

It is important to point out, as did Bandler and Grinder,[13] that this discussion of constraints on the model building processes is not meant to be a comprehensive presentation, nor is it meant to imply that there are distinct divisions between the three constraints. They actually overlap. The purpose of this book is to present the reader with *models* for perceiving, predicting, and influencing behavior. They are useful for these purposes even though they are inaccurate: A model merely *represents* what it is modeling.

Complex Equivalents

One example of overlapping constraints concerns lan-guage. Due to the influence of neurological and individual constraints, internal representations of language (social constraints) are different for everybody. For every word learned, everyone has a somewhat different internal experience. These specific experiences associated with words are called *complex equivalents.*[14] Usually the subtleties between people's understanding of words are irrelevant. However, there are words that sometimes lead to *mis*under-standing between people. Words like *love, relationship, partnership, fear, power, trust, respect,* and any expressions linked with a person's perception of himself and the environment are critical to the process of communication, as the example below demonstrates.

Complex Equivalents

It is important when you are learning the basic principles of effective communication to drop the assumption that you already know what words such as those listed above mean. Your "knowing" is based on your own model of the world which is also subject to the processes of generalization, deletion, and distortion, as well as to neurological, social, and individual constraints. Rather than presuming that your understanding of these words is the same as the speaker's, it is often advisable to ask for his own definitions. This may keep you from becoming trapped by your own model of the world. By more fully understanding what the speaker is saying, you are more likely to gain rapport and be more influential in your communication with him. Specific techniques for asking for a person's definitions of these words as well as some linguistic clues for when more information is needed are given in Chapter III.

Summary

I do not attempt to define what a human being
is, I describe what a human being *does.* (p. 30)
Bois, *The Art of*
Awareness

...we are looking for pragmatic redundancies; we know that they will not be simple, static magnitudes or qualities, but patterns analogous to the mathematical concept of function.... (p. 41)

> Watzlawick, et al.,
> *Pragmatics of Human Communication*

In dealing with communication, it is important to note the distinction made by Walzlawick, that *all* behavior is communication. There are actually two kinds of communicative behavior. One encompasses observable patterns of interaction, primarily speech and overt gestures. The other is less obvious communication that goes on *inside* each of us all the time. All communication, whether overtly exhibited or internally experienced, affects us in observable ways. It is the observation and utilization of specific communicative behaviors that make up the major theme of this book.

Once we begin to explore the ways we make sense of the myriad experiences we call "living," many behavioral patterns become evident. Grinder and Bandler's "human modeling processes" afford us an organizational basis from which to explore differences between what people experience (the territory) and how they make sense of those experiences (their map or model of the world).

Supported by evidence from neurological studies, we extend this model-building behavior to include three constraints: neurological, social, and individual. By understanding that these mechanisms are important in the creating of an individual's model and in that person's representation of "who" he is, we begin the first step in gaining the rapport and trust so important to influential and therapeutic communications. Recognizing that each person creates a different model of the world enables us to cherish rather than judge or fear those differences. It is those differences that make each of us unique and create the amazing and wonderful diversity of personality we encounter within and between societies.

We share a universal linguistic convention: understanding

presupposes consistencies in language at many levels. It is through these consistent patterns of behavior that we are able to survive in and perpetuate a society. These same behaviors provide clues as to how an individual creates not only joy and understanding but also pain and confusion in his daily life.

Some elements of communication are within our conscious control, but most are completely outside our conscious awareness. As we begin to attend to communication as a presentation of unique personal models, many of those idiosyncracies which produce miscommunication and misunderstanding become, instead, tools for even deeper and more profound communication. The more astute we become at seeing, hearing, and feeling the total messages being sent, the better able we will be to perceive what is really meant. This awareness will also enable us to better use our own channels of communication to express what we need and want, not only to others, but also *within* ourselves.

This book is a presentation of various models of human behavior. These models can be extremely useful as tools when used to understand, predict, and shape the human interactions we call communication. But these models can also be very limiting if we forget that they are not actually reality. We must keep in mind the idea stated so well by Edward T. Hall:

> All theoretical models are incomplete. By definition, they are abstractions and therefore leave things out. What they leave out is as important as, if not more important than, what they do not, because it is what is left out that gives structure and form to the system. (p. 14)
> *Beyond Culture*

CHAPTER II

THE COMMUNICATION
CATEGORIES MODEL

> Sorcerers say that we are inside a bubble. It is a
> bubble into which we are placed at the moment
> of our birth. At first the bubble is open, but then
> it begins to close until it has sealed us in. That
> bubble is our perception. We live inside that
> bubble all of our lives. And what we witness on
> its round walls is our own reflection.
>
> Don Juan, from Carlos
> Castaneda, *Tales of Power*

Representational Systems

Perception is an exciting area of study in the field of
psychology. As discussed in the previous chapter, because
neurological input forms the building blocks of our models of
the world, there are many different ways to describe the
process we call perception. What follows is based on the
neurological model presented in Chapter I.

There are five primary ways humans experience the world.
Barring neurological damage, we can see, feel, hear, smell,

and taste. Each one of these sensory inputs has physical places in our brains to which the experience is sent, processed, and recorded. This *assimilation* of the initial input transforms the experience into something different from the original stimulus. What we actually perceive are *re-presentations* or *models* of what each of our sensory organs transmits to us. These individual models of assimilation are called *representational systems.*[1]

At any moment we are receiving and processing input from all of our senses, even when we are not consciously aware of it. Each "slice out of time" is composed of the elements which make up the *4 - tuple (4T)* presented in Chapter I. Every 4T includes each of the representational systems: sight is the "visual" system (V); feeling is the "kinesthetic" system (K); hearing is the "auditory" system (A); and smell and taste make up the "olfactory" system (O).[2] The 4T is written like this:

$$\langle V \ K \ A \ O \rangle$$

In order to differentiate between experience of external origins and synthetic or internally generated experience, the subscripts *e* for *external* and *i* for *internal* can be used. For example, I may be reading a magazine and turn a page to see a full-color picture of a sailboat (V_e). This in turn may

External V; Internal K, A, O

instantly elicit the memory of the feeling of a boat rocking under my feet (K_i), the sound of sails slapping in the wind (A_i), and the smell and taste of the ocean (O_i). The 4T for that complete experience would be written like this:

$$\langle V_e K_i A_i O_i \rangle$$

To review briefly, the 4T is a model of one moment in time. It includes each of the four representational systems and can be written in formal notation as: $\langle V\ K\ A\ O \rangle$. The subscripts e and i identify whether the representation comes from external or internal origins. This formal shorthand can help make the observation and discussion of communicative behaviors easier and more concise.

The Digital System

During the process of building our models of the world, language and other social constraints are attached to our experiences. The collection of word symbols and the rules which govern their use make up a unique and distinct representational system. Unlike the systems in the 4T, the *digital system*, made up of language, is not an analog system: it is not directly related to any of our sensory organs. Language is the only system which can represent all of the other representational systems. It can create models of (re-present) each system including itself. There is evidence that this more recently evolved modeling tool may be subjugated to the analog systems, however. The following description from Watzlawick, et al.[3] demonstrates this relationship:

> Children, fools and animals have always been credited with particular intuition regarding the sincerity of human attitudes, for it is easy to profess something verbally, but difficult to carry a lie into the realm of the analogic.

The goal of this book is to increase your ability to detect and utilize patterns of behavior that occur both within an individual and between people as they interact. Language, the digital representational system, is able to re-present all of the systems used by people to create and communicate their experiences of the world. Because of this, it provides an especially effective tool for alerting an attentive listener to important information about a speaker's model of the world.

Differing patterns of word usage are demonstrated in the following five sentences. Take a moment to read each one carefully. Pay particular attention to how each one elicits a somewhat different subjective experience.

Sentence 1

I looked down from where I sat at the head of the long, dark, oak table, and it seemed to me that they should all know better than to think the thoughts I saw clearly reflected on their bright, smiling faces.

Sentence 2

I was suddenly aware of that helpless feeling again, that gnawing sensation in my belly, and, lowering my eyes, I knelt down gripping at the smooth, comforting folds of my robe.

Sentence 3

That rings a bell with me, too; it would be good if we could tune ourselves into your program without altering our tempo and thus create more harmonious relationships within the group.

Sentence 4

The salty sea breezes mixed with the sweet scent of delicate flowers, but the nearby marsh reeked of pungent, sulferous earth which kept threatening to spoil an otherwise savory afternoon.

Sentence 5

It is quite possible that the current situation could be improved, if not by moderating, then perhaps by rearticulating the response argument in order to preclude less desirable results.

Each of the above sentences utilizes one of the representational systems. Through the consistent use of certain words and phrases in each sentence, the reader is led into an experience — an "understanding" — which taps portions of his model of the world associated with his sensory systems. This is true except, of course, for the last sentence.

The first sentence, for example, illustrates the visual representational system. Many readers find that they can actually "see" the table, the faces, and the thoughts. By going through their own *personal history* — the collection of all past experiences stored in the mind — they create for themselves internal experiences similar to the one described. In the same way, most people are able to create "feelings" from the second sentence, which exemplifies the kinesthetic system. This creative construction of internal experiences in response to words plays a crucial role in the process of communication.

Emotions

The kinesthetic representational system includes several important distinctions. Sensory inputs from the body are classed as *somatic* sensations. These include the *exteroceptive* sensations of temperature, touch, and pain; *proprioceptive* sensations from deeper in our muscles, tendons, and joints which keep us informed as to body position, vibrations, and deep pain and pressure; and *visceral* sensations of pain and fullness from internal organs.

In our language, however, we have identified another kind of "feelings," those we call *emotions*. When someone says, "I was hurt," he may be talking about pressure or pain on his skin, or he may be talking about some "internal state" called an emotion.

Actually, the two meanings are very similar. To be "hurt" emotionally is a composite of several somatic sensations. For example, there may be a tightening around the eyes and face, changes in posture, stresses on deep muscle tissue, tendons, and joints, and often accompanying input from the viscera in the form of tightening or contractions. This sensory input is combined with other thought processes and is then labeled as emotional "hurt." Because of this close link with somatic sensations, it is useful to consider that those feelings we call emotions are actually *derived feelings,* or, in the formal notation: Kd.

The third sentence in the numbered examples elicits experiences associated with the auditory system, and the fourth the olfactory-gustatory system. Though taste and smell are two distinct sensory mechanisms, they are grouped together for simplicity. Generally, unless you are a gourmet chef or wine connoisseur, your model of the world probably does not contain as many distinctions in the olfactory representational system as in the other systems. In fact, the visual and kinesthetic appear to be two of the most often used systems in Western cultures.

The last of the numbered sentences is unique because none of the words presuppose any of the sensory-based systems. This is an example of purely digital information. In such a case, it is entirely up to the reader to "understand," using whatever system is best for him. This process will be explored in great detail in this chapter.

Olfactory-Gustatory Distinctions

Language is used to communicate various aspects of our experience of the world to each other. By creating internal, sensory-based experiences in response to the words we read or hear, we are each able to *understand* what is being said. However, this synthetic experience can also operate in ways which prevent us from experiencing fully what the speaker or writer intends to communicate. Because our understanding is internally generated, it is affected by the universal human modeling processes of generalization, deletion, and distortion. Because we each have unique models of the world, the following axiom must be considered important to the study of communication:

> The *meaning* of any communication is defined by the *response* it elicits.

Predicate Preference

When listening to a person talk, sometimes a pattern becomes evident, a pattern of *predicate preference*. These descriptive words and phrases — primarily verbs, adverbs and adjectives — often presuppose one of the representational systems. As you listen to a person talk over a period of time, you may discover that there are times when a majority of the predicates he uses refer to one system more often than any of the others. This person is choosing, usually at an unconscious level, to isolate one system from his ongoing "stream" of 4T's. Then, using the digital system, he identifies that system by the words he selects to communicate with. This is important, because it indicates to you *how* that person is making sense of his experience. It is a clue to the person's model of the world, and it also indicates what type of sensory experience he is most likely to notice.

Preferred Representational Systems

This more frequent use of one system over the others is called a person's *preferred representational system.*[4] Its use can be thought of as habitual, and it often becomes particularly evident during situations which are stressful for the individual. This system is usually the one a person makes the most distinctions in. It is the system used most often by him to consciously and unconsciously represent and understand his experiences. One excellent example of how the preferred systems operate is given by Roger Shepard, a Professor of Psychology at Stanford University. In describing his "creative thinking processes," Shepard states:

> That in all of these sudden illuminations my ideas took shape in a primarily visual-spatial form without. So far as I can introspect, any verbal intervention is in accordance with what has always been my preferred mode of thinking. . . .[5]

Another fine example of preferred representational systems took place while I was sitting with some friends one evening on a deck overlooking a beautiful stretch of the Pacific Ocean. Filled with the moment, we began to take turns describing our experiences. The following three quotations are more or less representative of what was actually said.

Susan

> I love the view. Look at the fantastic red and
> purple colors in the clouds where the sun just
> went down and how clearly they reflect in the
> water over there. . . .

In the above example, Susan's predicates consistently
reflect the visual representational system. Specifically, the
visual predicates are: verbs — "Look," "reflect"; adverbs —
"clearly"; adjectives — "red," "purple." Also nouns like
"view" and "colors" indicate the visual system. This
person's description of the moment can create a "picture" in
the listener's mind. It is an important indication of the part
of the experience that is most important to Susan. People
who consistently use this mode of expression will often use
phrases like: "I see what you mean," and, "Let me see if I can
remember."

Thomas

> Right now I'm feeling very warm, almost
> radiant, towards all of you. I feel as though I've
> been in touch with each of you today in a
> special way, and sitting here with you all so
> close enhances that feeling.

This person places a great deal of emphasis on feelings,
emotions and other kinesthetic aspects of the experience. The
kinesthetic predicates are: verbs — "feeling," "feel," "been in
touch," "sitting"; adverbs — "warm," "radiant," "close."
Common phrases used by people who speak from this system
are: "Can you handle it?" and, "I feel pretty comfortable with
the situation now."

Mark

> I was noticing how, as the sun went down,
> everyone's voice got quieter, almost as if the

change in the tone of the scenery was being
echoed by our voices. I like days like this; it
reminds me of a tune my father used to play on
the guitar. . . .

Auditory predicates characterize Mark's description. They
include verbs like "echoed," and "play" (the guitar) and
adverbs like "quieter." Other words auditory in nature are
"voice" and "tone." Someone with a highly developed
auditory representational system may make statements like:
"That shirt is too loud for me," and, "Does that sound good to
you?"

Leading by a Nose

In animals like dogs and cats, the olfactory
system is crucial for their survival. In humans,
however, it is less important. Though we
probably make fewer distinctions in this
system than in the others, it is very likely our
most efficient *lead system*. A lead system is the
representational system that is used to gain
access to information stored in our minds. For
example, we can search through our memories
visually, like flipping through a series of slides;
we can grope around, trying to get a feel for the
answer to a hard question; or we can stammer
as we desperately try to remember the name of
an important person by going through a series
of, "It sounds like _____, and rhymes with
_____"

Because olfactory input does not go through
the same neurological processing on the way to
the brain as the other systems,[6] it tends to
operate more efficiently as a lead system. This
system has also not escaped linguistic modeling. Several common phrases which utilized
the olfactory system are: "It's bitter cold
outside," and "That was tastefully done."

Use of representational systems is one of the ways people change their sensory input from the world into a model or a re-presentation of the world. Representational systems not only indicate the *process* by which individuals formally create their models but also provide us with a format by which we can understand how and what they experience. By listening carefully to the words people use, it is possible to identify patterns in their language which indicate preference for one representational system over the others. Preferred representational systems are one of the most systematic ways in which people's models of the world differ. As we continue to demystify the processes of communication we will attend to these differences.

Using the Language of the Representational Systems

In Chapter I it was suggested that everyone creates a model of the world and that due to differences in neurological, social, and individual constraints, everyone's model is different. Individual language patterns can assist us in determining what some of those differences are. Someone who occasionally says, "Yes, I see what you mean," is giving you a marvelous piece of information about how this person is making sense of what you are saying. Knowing this, you can frame your own language in such a way that you *match* that person's model. By using more visual predicates, you can help him to "see" even more "clearly" what you are talking about. By the same token, someone who says, "I don't quite grasp your meaning," may respond positively to a different linguistic pattern. Rather than trying to "paint a picture" for him with your words, it might be more effective to "grapple with the concepts" and "put them into pieces" that are "easier to get a handle on."

One way to think about preferred representational systems is to consider that each system has its own "language." This means that there are several different languages that are "foreign" to one another. By being able to understand and speak to a person using his own "language," you heighten the sense of rapport between you and pave the way for the trust that is so important to any close relationship.[7] Another way to think about predicate preference is to imagine how a blind person might perceive an elephant in comparison to a sighted person. You can be sure that their linguistic descriptions would demonstrate the differences.

Even though a person demonstrates a preference for one of the representational systems, it does not mean that he does not use the other systems too. On the contrary, we all use all of the systems all of the time. It has been my observation, however, that whether out of habit, in response to stressful situations, or in other areas of interaction, people tend to depend on their preferred system, the system in which they can make the most distinctions about the world. It also appears that, in some people, this system changes depending on the specific situation confronting them.

Stress

Fire engines clanged and wailed in the streets below, and people screamed unintelligible words from the buildings across the boulevard. The smell of smoke was getting more intense — that was probably what woke him up. Fire!

The image of burning buildings, flaming stairwells, and smoke-clogged hallways set him into a panic. He ran into the main hallway and started choking from the smoke he thought he could see there. He began looking frantically for a way out, trying to visualize where the fire escapes were.

Someone came up behind him and tapped him on the shoulder, saying, "Everyone's gone down the back way. Follow me.!" Then he ran off, leading the way, assuming he was being followed. But the panic-struck man didn't turn and follow. He was still busy trying to remember, trying to visualize where he had seen an escape route. In his frenzy, *he never even felt the touch nor did he hear the words* from behind him!

Often people under stress will turn to the representational system they trust the most. They may even delete other systems from their conscious awareness, thereby limiting their ability to respond. It is tragic because during just those times they need all the sensory input and all the awareness they can get! People coming into therapy who are under great stress in their lives are often extremely limited in their awareness of their problems and in their choices concerning how to behave. It is possible they are blocked by their inability to create new choices or to even perceive alternatives because the choices and perceptions lie outside the range of the system into which they have retreated.

The language of the representation systems can work for you in two ways. Besides indicating how a person is making sense of his experience, it can also provide an extremely effective method for gaining rapport with that person. This can be demonstrated by using the following illustration of a married couple who have come for counseling. Notice the linguistic patterns being used by the couple as they try to describe the "problem."

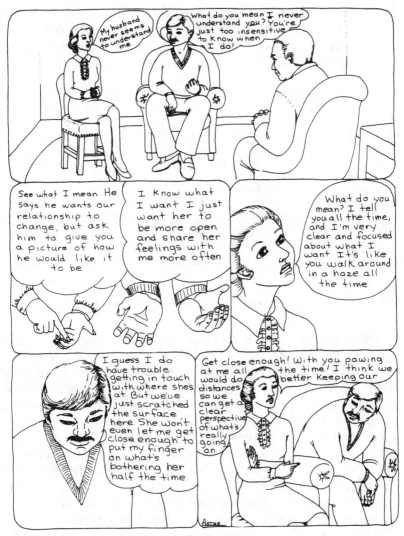

Let us imagine that the well-intentioned counselor decides to respond to the above situation by turning to the woman and saying, "It's obvious that you are upset. What are your feelings telling you? Speak from your guts; share your emotions with us." In this hypothetical example, the woman might reply with: "Well, I don't really know what you mean. It just seems that everything I do is wrong. Things just aren't what I pictured they would be when I got married, and my husband doesn't even seem to care!"

The key to this interaction is in the woman's response to the counselor. She is being very honest with him when she says she really doesn't know what he means. For him to persist in asking her to "contact those feelings" or to "get in touch with her emotions" may lead to a counterproductive session. This is a situation where using the same "language" as the client could prove invaluable. Once he gains rapport with the woman, once she has the sense that he really "understands" her, then he can begin to systematically alter his language, "translating" the language of one system into another in order to effectively communicate with both her and her husband. The next step is to *teach* the couple to speak and understand each other's language. This can be done either overtly by talking about the use of predicates or through example, by simply continuing to "translate" whenever appropriate.

Functional Differences

It is perhaps the "mismatching" of predicates that accounts in part for the confounding fact that "great" therapists can work miracles with some clients but are almost totally ineffective with others. Preferred representational systems may also play an important role in a therapist's choice of which psychotherapeutic techniques to study. For example, the more traditional psychotherapies rely heavily on the client's ability to digitalize — to talk about — and to visualize various experiences. Some of the humanistic approaches, on the other hand, identifying feelings or emotions as the medium through which to achieve change. These are *functional differences*, differences which, on the positive side, enable individuals with different models of the world to seek out and work within a system that best suits their own.

The sooner you begin to match the client's predicates, to speak his own language, the more rapidly therapy can progress. This is true in any situation where a close relationship is being fostered, whether you are a therapist, a teacher, or an office manager. The ability to adapt your own language to the predicates of others is as important in a close intimate relationship like a family as it is in situations where people must work together. The following illustration

demonstrates what sometimes happens when two people who come together in the work environment speak two different "languages."

The result of changing your language to match the person you are talking with is two-fold. First, the person begins to feel more at ease with you and is more likely to trust you: "Ah! Someone who really understands me!" Second, you create an environment in which miscommunication is much less likely to occur. This is because you leave no room for contradictions between what you say or ask for and the internal experience — model of the world — of the person you are talking with. Also, because you are more "like" him in his experience, it is easier for him to "like" you.

Representational System Hierarchies

A person's preferred representational system is the one in which he generally makes the most number of distinctions about the world. One way to determine which system a person prefers is to give him the *Representational System Bias Test* (see Appendix B at the end of this book). By tallying the scores as shown, you can determine a person's *representational system hierarchy*.[8] His preferred system will have a higher score than his *secondary system,* and so on. This "ranking" of a person's representational systems has some important ramifications. As demonstrated in previous examples, difficulties can arise when two people who need to communicate each have different preferred systems. This is especially true when the difference between the scores is large as in the example below.

Person A: V - 7   K - 20   A - 10   D - 13
Person B: V - 20   K - 6   A - 9   D - 15

Person A's *least* valued system (the visual
system) is person B's *preferred* system and vice
versa. In terms of being able to "speak the
same language," their representational system
hierarchies already pose a formidable obstacle
to effective communication!

The Communication Categories Model

Predicate preference is only one indication of how people
are representing or experiencing the world. In this section we
will explore other ways people indicate their preferred
systems, many of which can be observed before they even
open their mouths.

Caution: Generalization Ahead

In the discussion about human modeling
processes, one of the primary areas discussed was the process of *generalization* which is important to our
ability to learn a great complexity
of information and new behaviors.
However, generalizations may also become a source of pain for an individual by
limiting both behavior and perception in nonproductive ways.

The meta principles of
communication and change
presented in this handbook
are based on generaliza-
tions — behavioral patterns
within an individual's sphere of activity as
well as consistencies of interaction between
members of a society. But these are only
generalizations; they are only *models* of
behavior.

It is important to remember a point made earlier: Everyone has a different map or model of reality. *We are all different.* What is presented on the following pages are generalizations about people that are only useful when they assist us in more efficient and effective communication. *Be wary* of the potential to become limited by these same generalizations. It is better to trust what you see, hear, and feel than to rely on a highly generalized model of behavior. Remember: If the model doesn't fit, *don't use it.*

Based in part on the work of family therapist Virginia Satir[9] and the human behavior modelers Bandler and Grinder,[10] I have consolidated into a model four basic *communication categories*. This model is organized around the four preferred representational systems. These are the visual system, the kinesthetic system, the auditory tonal system, and the digital system.

There is an efficient shorthand that will be used throughout this book to identify each of the communication categories. Because the model is organized around the four representational systems, the following labels will be used. A person demonstrating characteristics associated with the visual communication category will be called a "visual." One who is operating within the kinesthetic modality will be called a "kino." Someone exhibiting behaviors associated with the auditory system will be called a "tonal," and a person operating out of the digital system will be called a "digital."

These labels can be used in two ways. One way is to describe an individual who habitually represents experience with one of the systems more often than the others. The other way is to describe how an individual is representing his experience in a particular situation. In this case, the label identifies the *dominant* mode of behavior in that particular situation. In the illustration on page 44, for example, we could say that the man is being a "kino," and the woman is being a "visual."

The Communication Categories Model
Outline

The following list represents the specific areas of behavior covered by the communication categories model. These behaviors are different for each of the four systems and are described in detail in the text. A complete chart with specific behaviors listed under the "visual," "kino," "tonal," and "digital" systems is presented in Appendix C.

1. Predicates which presuppose a representational system (preferred system).
2. Postural characteristics.
3. Body "types" and movements.
4. Lip size.
5. Breathing patterns.
6. Voice tonality, speed, and tempo.
7. Eye elevation in relation to others.
8. Rules for looking while listening.
9. Satir categories.
10. Meta model violations: linguistic idiosyncracies.
11. Meta model ill-formed meanings.
12. Accessing cues.

It is important to keep in mind throughout this book the warning previously issued. This model and the labels associated with it are only generalizations about people. They delete a great deal of information; this is a part of how they are supposed to function. They can make it easier for us to perceive, understand, and predict behavior. However, as mentioned in a popular text on psychology, "Labels intended to be merely descriptive may also come to be regarded as explanations of the problem."[12] They should never be used in a way which might interfere with either our *perceptions of* or our *behaviors toward* those we have labeled. The examples in the sections which follow are intended to simplify the task of detecting behavioral patterns. However, remember that it is always best to use your own observations when a model doesn't fit.

Posture and Body Cues

Although heredity plays an important part in creating the physical appearance we each display, psychologists have long recognized the relationship between personality — our model of the world — and physical characteristics.[13] Because these physical qualities are externally exhibited, they are communicative signals which can be useful tools in the process of demystifying communication.

"Visuals"

"Mrs. McCulvary was my third grade teacher. I remember her well if not fondly. She was so skinny and tall, our nickname for her was ostrich, although that could also be because of the colorful "plumage" she sometimes wore. She always seemed to look down her nose at everyone, and she had a tendency to screech whenever she talked to us."

The above description of the fictional Mrs. McCulvary is a good example of some of the characteristics often displayed by "visuals." It is not unusual for the habitual "visual" to be thin, although you will occasionally run across a very fat or obese "visual" (see "Body: Brief Analysis" on page 53). They usually stand erect with their shoulders held up or back. People who are being "visual" will keep their necks straight and erect, matching their bodies. They often appear to "lead with their chin" when they walk, and their motions can be described as stiff or jerky. Habitual "visuals" will often have a smaller rib extension than individuals from the other categories, and they tend to breathe more into the upper portion of the chest. It is not uncommon for the "visual" to speak in a fast, clear or distinct way with a higher pitch than people operating from the other categories.

Figure 2 - 1 is an illustration of some of the physical characteristics described above. Some of these postural and tonal behaviors can be observed in individuals operating out of the visual system even though their preferred system is not visual. This would include breathing and movement, although the visual body type and rib cage extension would most likely be demonstrated only by a habitual "visual."

This ability to operate in systems other than the preferred system is true for all of the communication categories.

Figure 2 - 1

"Kinos"

Think of the image evoked by Santa Claus. He is always depicted as a soft and rather round man with rosy cheeks and a flowing white beard. When he laughs, his whole belly jiggles, and the feelings he elicits are warm and happy.

The figure of Santa is an appropriate example of a "kino." The habitual "kino" generally has more flesh on his body than individuals from the other categories, although they tend not to be obese. When communicating from this modality, individuals will often demonstrate a rounding of the shoulders, and they sometimes bend slightly forward as they speak and listen. Their motions tend to be flowing and loose; how else would Santa get down the chimney! Habitual "kinos" often have a larger rib extension compared to the other categories. When operating from this modality, people tend to breathe into the lower portion of the lungs. The tonality of a "kino" might be generalized as having soft or airy qualities with a slower tempo and lower tone and volume than the other categories. Figure 2 - 2 illustrates this category.

Figure 2 - 2

Body: Brief Analysis

If you think in terms of the aspect of experience the habitual "kino" or "visual" is paying attention to, the structure of their bodies begins to make sense. When operating from the visual modality, a person becomes dissociated or disconnected from bodily experiences. This is because it is primarily the visual portions of the environment that command his attention. Physical demands such as hunger (or fullness!) often go unnoticed, and, though habitual "visuals" tend to be slimmer than people whose preferred system is kinesthetic, they can also become obese. Unlike the "visuals," habitual

54

"kinos" are more alert to bodily needs and comforts, including hunger and eating, so their frames tend to fill out. Also, where a "visual" will wear sharp, well coordinated and tailored clothing, a "kino" is more likely to wear soft and comfortable knits and fabrics.

Again, these are generalizations. We all have the ability to "be" any of the communication categories at different times. What is offered here are patterns of observable behavior, consistencies from which we can effectively predict specific styles of communication and portions of experience people are likely to be most aware of.

"Tonals"

It appears that, at least in the United States and other Western cultures, the proportion of habitual "tonals" is small

Figure 2 - 3

in relation to the other categories. Because of this, it is more difficult to make accurate generalizations about them. My experience with the few I have met leads me to believe that their physiques vary but tend toward the slim rather than the obese. A common communicative posture for this group as shown in Figure 2 - 3 is having the arms folded across the chest with the head tilted down and to the side, perhaps to listen. When they speak, they maintain more control over the auditory portion of communication than most people. In order to maintain this control over their reproduction of tonal aspects of their speech, they need to have a full range of breathing. They tend, therefore, to have larger rib cages than "visuals" and to utilize their lungs more fully.

"Digitals"

A person who is communicating from the digital modality generally speaks in a clipped, crisp monotone. Since variations in tone are relatively unimportant to them, the habitual "digital" exhibits breathing patterns more like

Figure 2 - 4

those of a "visual," that is, higher up in the chest. The digital system is based on language, a behavior which is acquired as a person matures. A "digital" person, like a "visual," is dissociated from his feelings. Since faculty with language comes somewhat later in life than visual, tonal, and kinesthetic abilities, it may be that a person becomes "digitalized" in response to some environmental situation. Most "digitals" that I have observed have physical body types similar to a "kino's." This suggests the adoption of the digital system as a means of coping (through dissociation) with feelings which may not be pleasant. Figure 2 - 4 illustrates some of the qualities of a "digital."

One interesting characteristic which seems to correlate with a person's communication category is the size of the lips. This is especially true of the lower lip. You may find it interesting to match this phenomena with your own observations. Visually oriented persons are often character-ized by rather thin, tight lips. People operating out of the kinesthetic category usually demonstrate fuller, softer lips. "Tonals" and "digitals" vary, however, the latter tending more toward thinner and tighter lips.

Voice: Brief Analysis

Characteristics of voice associated with each of the communication categories are related to breathing patterns. For example, where "vis-uals" tend to breathe higher up in the chest, it makes sense that the volume of air taken in will be less than that taken in by a "tonal," who utilizes more of the lungs. With so much less volume, the "visual" needs to speak faster in order to say as much with each breath. It may be that they often talk with a higher pitched voice because this cuts off more of the flow of air crossing the vocal chords, enabling them to conserve air.

"Kinos," on the other hand, in order to breathe as deeply as they do, must open up the windpipe more. This can give their voices a more breathy or airy quality when they speak. This relaxation of the throat may also add to the tendency to speak at a slower pace than the other categories.

Remember, we all have the ability to "be" any one or even a combination of each of these categories at different times. Even the habitual "visual," "kino," "tonal," and "digital" can fluctuate, making body type or build unreliable. Rather than depending on a highly generalized model, it is always better to maintain open and clear perceptual channels and trust your own *experience*.

Other Behavioral Cues

There are certain patterns of behavior which seem to be consistent within each of the communication categories, particularly in stressful situations. A person who is being "visual" pays most attention to the visual aspects of an interaction. This includes both the facial expressions and other gestures and movements of those around him as well as his own internally generated visual imagery. In order to adequately attend to someone he is talking to, it is important for the "visual" to situate himself so that he can clearly see as much of that person as possible. Because of this, "visuals" tend to keep more physical distance between themselves and others, at least enough distance to be able to see most, if not all, of those with whom they are communicating. Because they often place themselves at an angle that will give them the best vantage-point, usually somewhat above others, they often appear to be "looking down on" everyone else.

People who are operating out of the kinesthetic communication category rely heavily on feelings in order to understand and make sense out of what is happening around them. They are most likely to place themselves whenever possible in a position in which they can be close enough to actually touch the people they are talking with. Just as the "visual" gains information about a speaker by observing subtle movements, muscular tension and relaxation, the "kino" gains the same information through touch and close proximity. Though people operating out of either of the systems have the ability to use any representational system, they will tend to rely upon their preferred system for most of their information.

As you can imagine, there is great potential for discomfort and miscommunication between two individuals communicating from these two different communication categories. Where the "visual" needs distance so as to get a "clear picture" of the process, the "kino" wants to get close enough to insure a "good connection." However, the moment the "kino" pushes past the comfortable distance range for the "visual," the "visual" goes into stress. This stress is communicated — usually analogically through a tightening of the skeletal muscles and a strain in the voice tonality — to the "kino" who responds by also going into stress. Of course, in the stress situation, the "kino" will want even more "contact," and the demands for closeness increase resulting in even more stress for the "visual."

The processes described above all go on almost totally outside the awareness of the individuals involved. This is a common pattern found in couples who come in for counseling. The results are often verbalized in the following way:

> Husband: "I never feel as if we have really connected, especially when we argue. I feel like there's a great distance between us."
>
> Wife: "He never seems to get the whole picture. He's always invading my space and 'pawing' at me while we're trying to have a serious conversation."
>
> (Of course, these roles are just as often reversed.)

Anthropologist Edward Hall, previously cited, has noticed similar patterns within whole cultures. In one article, Hall points out that of the cultures he has studied, the Arabs prefer a much closer "conversational distance" than any of the others, especially compared to the typical "American." His description of their behaviors is an interesting blend of social constraints (see Chapter I) and representational systems.

> Overall, what they're doing is coding, sort of synthesizing, their reactions. They say to themselves, "How do I feel about this person?" In contemporary American terms: "What kind of vibes am I getting from him?" They are also responding to smell and to the thermal qualities of the other person. We talk about someone with a warm personality. This is literally true, and there is [also] a very cold fish. This is the person who draws heat from you. So they're picking up thermal, olfactory, and kinesthetic cues also. A lot of touching goes on during conversations in the Middle East. . . .[14]

General positioning in relation to others for "tonals" and "digitals" is less consistent, though they will both tend to place themselves close enough to hear. Also, for "digitals," both physical and eye contact are avoided. It may be that visual input distracts the "digital" from the high concentration necessary to maintain control over his verbal output while a touch has the potential to "reconnect" him with the feelings from which he is dissociated. Where "digitals" and "visuals" will gaze above the heads of others — "thinking" and "searching for the correct words to say" — "tonals" tend to avert their eyes down and away from the speaker, also in order to keep from being distracted, though more often during listening than speaking.

Touching

Those who habitually communicate from the digital category can be thought of as having learned a particular coping pattern. Especially under stress, these individuals appear to dissociate from their feelings, emotions, and even from an awareness of the body. They do this by "going into their heads" and filling the void with a flood of words.

Touching people who are behaving in this manner, who are communicating from this category, may suddenly remind them of their bodies and of the feelings and emotions from which they have dissociated themselves. It may be for this reason that they have learned to keep some physical distance between themselves and others. This is an important point to remember when communicating with "digitals," and in some cases with "visuals" as well. A touch can be utilized to distract these individuals from their ongoing thought processes. Touching can also be used to assist them in reconnecting with their bodies and emotions.

Rules for Listening

There appear to be certain *rules for listening* associated with each of the communication categories. Though these rules vary from one culture to another,[15] for each category they remain consistent within the culture. The rules deal with direct eye contact and are described below. Once learned, these rules can provide you with more understanding of and control over the communication process.

A person operating out of the visual system must be able to *see* the speaker in order to easily understand what is being said. This need is then generalized or "projected" onto others with whom the "visual" is communicating. The "look-to-listen" rule can be stated thus:

"Since I must look at you in order to hear and understand you, then you must look at me in order for me to know that you are hearing and understanding me."

In the case of "digitals" and especially with "tonals," the look-to-listen rule is reversed. Since visual input is a distraction to their ability to hear and understand, "tonals" and "digitals" may state the looking rule as follows:

> "I must look away in order to hear and understand."

This rule is not projected onto others, however, like the look-to-listen rule of the "visuals." The "tonal" and "digital" do not need to look to see whether or not the person listening is looking, since the visual component is not the important element for them in the communication process.

The contradiction between the two rules for listening has many ramifications. How often have you encountered or participated in the scene illustrated below in which the angry adult takes the child's chin in hand, saying, "Look at me when I'm talking to you!"? This is often an example of conflict between the look-to-listen and must-look-away rules.

In stressful situations, "digitals" and "tonals" are usually less comfortable trying to understand what is being said to them if they are being "forced" to make eye contact. This is also generally true for someone operating out of the kinesthetic model. What these people see distracts their attention from the representational system in which they make the most distinctions. The other systems simply fail to provide information in ways that are as easily utilized by them as the information which matches their preferred system.

There is another difficulty which arises when someone with the look-to-listen rule also believes that if someone looks away while speaking, it means that he is lying.[16] In the situation illustrated above, if the child is not operating out of the visual system, he may find it difficult to talk while looking directly at the adult. Again, due to the visual distraction, the child might have trouble "thinking" in his habitual system without looking away.[17] This could create dire consequences if the adult thinks the child is lying because he keeps looking away.

In Chapter I a somewhat different eye-contact rule was discussed regarding social constraints (see page 34). In that example, it was demonstrated how a lack of knowledge or understanding of the social rule governing direct eye contact could lead to conflict between individuals from different social backgrounds. It is important to recognize that differences also exist between individuals in a homogeneous social group. This is because people tend to orient themselves to aspects of experience that correlate to their preferred representational systems. When you can identify these differences between people, you can more easily "tune in to," "see clearly," and "connect" with other people's models of the world. This is one of those "magical" qualities of very effective communicators. By identifying and then using these differences, you will run less of a risk of making the mistake of judging another's behavior solely by the standards of your own model. You can more easily "bridge the gap" between yourself and your clients, students, co-workers, and anyone else with whom it is important for you to communicate.

Satir Categories

The following behavioral patterns come from an unusually gifted people helper, Virginia Satir. In her book, *Peoplemak-*

ing, Satir identifies four "postural stances" that people often take during the communication process.[17] In their exaggerated form, says Satir, ". . . so exaggerated that nobody could miss it," (p. 63) these stances form the *Satir Categories*, so called after the works of Bandler and Grinder.[18] These postures are associated with the communication categories as follows.

Under stress, visual representers tend to take on the postural characteristics of Satir's "blamer." That is, they take on an aggressive stance, pointing their fingers at the person they are talking to and using expressions like: "You always do that. Why can't you do anything right?" (A more complete presentation of word-patterns used by each of the communication categories is given in the next chapter.)

People who are operating as "kinos" assume the "placater" stance, especially under stress. Satir pictures a person down on one knee, hands turned palms-up as if "begging for forgiveness." Phrases associated with this posture are: "I feel so bad about making you mad at me. I just can't do anything right. Please forgive me."

"Digitals" take the "computer" posture. Crossing their arms and avoiding eye contact by looking over everyone's head, it is easy to become lost in their superlogical non-sensory-based language. Again, particularly in stressful situations, these individuals use expressions like: "The correct procedure in such cases, especially if one concurs with the current arguments, might be suggested as being statistically more appropriate to the former rather than the latter remarks."

Although the "tonal" person sometimes takes on the "computer" characteristics, he is more likely to assume the role of Satir's "distracter." If he overhears two people talking who are just on the verge of getting angry (remember, he is extremely sensitive to their tonal cues, so his "timing" is exquisite!) he may suddenly interrupt them by asking for the time of day, by turning on the TV or radio too loud, or by some other distracting action. Under stress, as in the above situation, the "tonal" is likely to say such things as, "It's good that people like you can keep such a harmonious relationship. It must be nice to know you're being thought of.

Where's the TV Guide?"

Satir points out that there is often a difference between what the person's body appears to communicate and what is actually "going on inside." Where the "computer" stance seems to express "calm, cool, and collected," says Satir, this person may actually be feeling very vulnerable. The "placater" says "I'm helpless" with his posture while inside he is feeling completely worthless. The "blamer" who is communicating "I am the boss around here" with his stance is feeling lonely and unsuccessful, while the constantly irrelevant "distracter" with his unbalanced stance may be feeling that nobody cares.

Each of the Satir stances can also be exhibited in less obvious ways. Hand gestures often indicate one of the postures. The pointing of a finger or an upturned hand may indicate the blaming and placating postures respectively. Especially when combined with key phrases like "You always. . .," and "I'm sorry. . .," these gestures can be important indications about how a person is relating to the world and to others around him. Detection of such patterns can assist you in gaining rapport with the people you live and work with while aiding you in understanding how people get "stuck" in communicative patterns that consistently fail to give them what they want and need.

Another Warning

The previous generalizations are not to be considered universally applicable. They are presented as useful tools for describing patterns in people's behavior. When a behavior is identified as fitting in with several other patterns, it can be used to help you understand that person's model of the world and can assist you in gaining the trust and rapport necessary for effective communication. These generalizations are only models and as such contain all the limitations inherent in any model. Use them when and where they apply, and discard them whenever they don't fit.

Summary

In this chapter, stress was mentioned in relation to a person's preferred representational system. What makes it so important is the effect it has on an individual's perceptions and behavior. As demonstrated with the story about the panic-stricken man, individuals under stress tend to turn to the representational system in which they make the most distinctions. This coping behavior, likely learned early in life, proved itself useful in enough situations to warrant its being maintained. The insidious thing about this kind of strategy for coping is that it is during stressful situations that people should have the greatest number of distinctions, as much information about their environment as possible. Ironically, it is during these very times of need that people choose (unconsciously) to adopt the limiting patterns of their preferred systems, often to the exclusion of the other systems.

When people walk into a therapist's office for counseling, it is usually because they have only very limited resources at their disposal. People often seek counseling because they are suffering the stresses associated with emotional pain or with the problems of dealing with a complex society. Recognizing people's limitations can be the first step in assisting them in discovering alternatives, new choices of perception and behavior. This is true in many different settings, from the classroom to the business office.

Your ability to identify and use the same representational system being used by those you work and live with will assist you in developing and maintaining a high level of effective communication. Determining the communication categories that these people use in various situations can help you gain their trust while enabling you to obtain the information necessary in order to assist them in making changes they want and need. This is truly the "magic" of powerful and effective communication.

When a person communicates with you, he presents you with information about how he has created his model of the world. This includes data about how and where some of the limits were built in to his model. With this information, you are not only able to *pace* his experience (gain/maintain rapport), you are also able to *lead* him in changing his perceptions and behaviors that are limiting and painful. This can be done verbally as well as nonverbally by utilizing all the analog systems of body posture, breathing, voice tonality, etc. The example which follows will demonstrate some of these techniques.

A highly visual person has come in for an initial interview. You know this from a combination of body posturing, build, lip size, clothing, predicate usage and other cues. You already know that one of his rules for communicating is that it is necessary to look in order to understand what another person is saying. If you were to turn away or listen by diverting your head as many people do, he might accuse you of not paying attention. This poor pace could be compounded further if you placed yourself too close and "invaded his space." Remember that visually oriented people are generally more comfortable when they can see you from a distance in order to get "the whole perspective."

By accepting this person's rules, by matching his predicates, in essence, by operating out of his model of the world, you begin to pave the road for a successful relationship. You can *mirror* various aspects of this person's communication category by matching your body posture, tonality, predicates, and by obeying the rules associated with that system. This will sometimes enable you to detect areas of pain and limits to this person's perception that would otherwise have remained hidden from you. At the same time you demonstrate "acceptance" by mirroring, you provide the person with the opportunity to *see, hear,* and *feel* himself in ways which are usually outside of his conscious awareness. As long as the rapport is maintained, you can utilize this subtle form of *feedback.* For example, you can lead the person to a more comfortable or functional place by simply *modeling* those changes in yourself. By changing his "reflection" in this way, the person has the opportunity to actually experience new choices at a deep, unconscious level, to "try them on" so to speak. As long as you are open to subtle changes in the person you are working with, you can immediately tell whether or not the changes are appropriate for him.

These are just a few of the ways in which this information can be utilized. As you learn and experience the subtle patterns of communication covered in this book, you may find yourself generating more and more innovative applications in many different situations.

A complete chart of all the behavioral characteristics associated with each of the communication categories is given in Appendix C.

CHAPTER III

THE META MODEL

If he is indeed wise [the teacher] does not bid
you enter the house of his wisdom, but rather
leads you to the threshold of your own mind.
Kahlil Gibran
The Prophet

The Digital Representational System

Symbolic Representation

The digital system, language, is the *symbolic* representation of experience. It is the only system which can represent all the other representational systems as well as being able to represent itself. Not directly related to any of our sensory organs, it is so unique that it warrants special attention. The historical importance of this system is discussed by Samuels and Samuels in their book *Seeing with the Mind's Eye*. As they put it:

> With the development of language and a
> written system for recording it, rational
> thought came to dominate. Words came to
> function as labels, allowing man to detach
> himself from his experience and analyze it....

tion, law and order, the development of philosophical and moral systems and the growth of mathematics and the sciences. As knowledge and communication increased people began to live out highly specialized social roles, carrying the sense of separation and alienation from nature to its extreme. (p. 12-13)

Such a powerful tool, the digital system! As with the other systems, it is not only an indicator of how a person creates his model of the world, but it also serves to enhance as well as limit perception. The discussion of social constraints (Chapter I) described how our ability to name something affects how we perceive it. In one example, the Eskimos' ability to name over seventy different kinds of snow was shown to be very important to their survival in the harsh northern climates. Only with their specific linguistic (digital) background is it possible to perceive the variations in the quality of snow indicated by their vocabulary.

Built into the encoding element of our linguistic processes is what we might call a *perceptual enhancer*. Once a linguistic symbol has been assigned to a specific experience, it becomes a discrete, manipulatable element that is differentiated from the surrounding environment or experience. The powerful effect of language is discussed by the general semanticist J. Samuel Bois in his book *The Art of Awareness*. He says on page 19:

> We see the world through the meshes of that human-made filter; we project on the world of phenomena the relations that we have learned to observe among the parts of speech; we interpret what is happening in terms of the logic of cause-effect that is embedded in our grammar.

Analog-Digital: The Computer Metaphor

There are two kinds of computers in common usage today. A *digital* computer, like a calculator, functions by transforming both the instructions and the data into numbers (symbols). These arbitrarily assigned symbols make possible the compilation or manipulation of information. Digital computers are often equated with logical functions and can demonstrate such relationships as "if...then" and the simple negation "not."

The *analog* computer operates on a program through which it runs information (input) in order to obtain results. This *process* orientation enables it to work with and measure quantities on an continuum such as intensity, weight, or turns of a wheel. From a bathroom scale or slide rule to the sophisticated guidance system of a rocket, the key to the analog computer is its manipulations of the analogs of data. These analogs are the similarities between data and its representations (like the number of turns of the numbered wheel on the bathroom scale), and these similarities are directly related to the data.

In the "human computer," both systems function conjointly. The differences, however, are important. The key to digital expression (language) is the *arbitrary* assignment of word-symbols to things or processes. There is no necessary connection between the name and the thing named. On the contrary, analog, by definition, means that something is similar to something else. Therefore, we can expect that analogic "language" or communication will more closely relate to what it is about.

For example, if we hear the word "eat" in an unfamiliar language, we are not likely to understand it. It is merely an arbitrarily assigned (digital) symbol for a common behavior. If, however, the person pantomimes the behavior (eating), that is, uses analogic communication, the meaning is much more likely to be understood.

But where analogic communication is more universal (and more "primitive"[1]), it is also limited in some very important ways. Since analogic communication can only portray a thing or an action, it cannot portray a thought or idea and is therefore unable to portray negation. Only the more abstract and versatile digital representation system can express negation. The digital system can also convey time and number manipulations which analog systems cannot.

Another limitation is that of ambiguity. A smile (analog) can come from an experience of pleasure or an experience of pain ("Grin and bear it"). A shrug of the shoulders can mean "I give up," "I don't care," or "I don't know." Just as with the analogic computer, there is always some error in translation, and in human analog systems there are no qualifiers to indicate which message is implied.[2]

By understanding the value of the mechanisms involved in the process of affixing labels to our experiences, we can become more alert to some of the effects these labels have on our perception. It is not unusual to judge behavior by its appearance, attaching a name or label to it and more or less "reifying" it. This tends to halt or at least limit future observations of the behavior's *effects*. Dr. Palazzoli talks about this problem in the book *Paradox and Counterparadox*. What she and her team of researchers discovered working with schizophrenic families was that *appearance* is not necessarily a valid indication of the *meaning* of a behavior. They write:

For example, if a patient appeared to be sad, we concluded he *was* sad, and we went so far as to try to understand *why* he was sad, inviting and encouraging him to speak to us about his sadness.

Linguistic Deconditioning

Taking their understanding one step further, Dr. Palazzoli and her colleagues began to explore the *function* of the client's behavior not only within the family system but also with the therapists themselves. Through a process they call *linguistic deconditioning,* they began to change their perception of the client's behavior from one of *being,* as in "He is (being) sad," to one of *seeming* or *showing,* as in "He is showing sadness," or "He seems sad."

From this vantage point, it is much easier to observe the *effects* of the behavior rather than to dwell on the *causes* of the behavior. It can be much more useful to define the meaning of a behavior or communication by its ultimate effects on those around the communicator. This is especially important with some forms of analog communication.

The Meta Model: Overview

In 1975 Richard Bandler and John Grinder published a book which outlined their now popular Meta Model.[3] This is a linguistic (digital) tool which has proven extremely useful in therapeutic as well as other settings. It is based on the observation that human behavior, especially linguistic behavior, is rule-governed. The same processes of generalization, deletion, and distortion used in creating our models of reality are also used in the creation of our linguistic representations of experience.

As it is presented here, the Meta Model includes several distinctions not in the original, and the format has been altered. The basic assumptions still apply, however. Since it is a linguistic tool, the Meta Model relies on the natural intuitions of any native speaker of the English language.[4]

In any communication, the spoken or written language, called the *surface structure* (SS), provides the listener with a rich variety of information about the speaker. It indicates how that person makes sense of the world, how he distorts his perceptions, and when and where those distortions occur. Predicates, for example, may indicate his preferred representational system. The surface structure can also indicate when and what kinds of experiences the speaker systematically leaves out of his representation of the world. By assisting the speaker in "reconnecting" with the unspoken portion of his digital representation of experience, called the *deep structure* (DS), you begin a process of exploration. This process can fill in gaps of understanding that may occur between you and assist the speaker in recognizing and confronting limitations to growth and experience he may not even have known existed.

Transformational Grammar

A contemporary school of linguistics[5] proposes a relationship between what is spoken or written by an individual and some deeper internal linguistic representation. The production of a sentence, the actual sound or written sequence of symbols and phrases, is called the *surface structure* (SS). The *deep structure* (DS) is also a system of symbols and phrases, but it is much more complex and abstract. The DS is the complete linguistic representation of a person's experience which might be considered the intent or the thought behind the SS sentence.

The theory is that the DS is transformed into SS by a series of rules. Transformational grammarians say that the DS and the SS are related by certain formal operations which conform to the concepts of generalizations, deletion and distortion covered in Chapter I.

Meta Model Violations

Any time you are reading or listening to a person speak and you find yourself having to "go inside" to understand what is being said, it is a pretty good indication that you have experienced what is called a "Meta Model violation." The fact that you are confused and need to internally generate information that is missing from or distorted in the speaker's SS is a cue that your intuitive processes as a native speaker are being utilized. This is a valuable process because it allows the speaker/writer to share a great deal of information rapidly without needing to fill in all the missing pieces. However, the same process may drastically limit the speaker's ability to express what he really means. A person's language can also indicate areas where he has limits on his ability to perceive the full richness of certain experiences. The result of such limitations and distortions may be that the speaker has few choices about how to feel or behave in certain situations.

Meta Model Responses

What the Meta Model does is make explicit those semantic and syntactic contexts, those expressions in which *Meta Model violations* occur. Once they can be systematically recognized, there are specific *Meta Model responses* which you can use to recover deleted material and to assist the speaker in reconnecting with his deep structure. Reconnecting with the fullest linguistic representation of a person's experience can aid him in understanding how certain generalizations, deletions and distortions cause pain and limit choice and perception. This paves the way for healthy growth and positive change.

The Meta Model is a set of eight linguistic distinctions which can be grouped into three categories. The first category, *Gathering Information*, begins the process of uncovering and exploring specific portions of the speaker's experience which are missing from his surface structure or which are presented in a distorted form. The second category, *Expanding Limits*, provides you with tools to assist the speaker in defining and then expanding the boundaries or limitations of his model of the world. This self-exploration assists the speaker in gaining more choices in both behavior and perception. The final category, *Changing Meanings*, continues the process of growth and expansion by exploring with the speaker how he understands himself and his relationship with the people around him and with the world in general.

Meta Model Diagram #1

The deep structure is the most complete linguistic representation that a person could give to experience. This is symbolized by the larger form below. The deep structure includes the boundary line and all the space contained within it.

The surface structure is the portion of the deep structure expressed by an individual when he speaks or writes. It is represented by the shaded portion of the larger form. Notice in the illustration below how the "shape" of the SS conforms to the "shape" of the DS. Since the transformational processes of creating the SS from the DS are essentially the same as the processes we use to create our models of reality, the SS is an invaluable indicator of how the speaker perceives the world around him. It is through the SS that we gain clues about the rest of the speaker's model. With the aid of the first category of Meta Model responses to violations, we gain more information about the unshaded portion of the model below, the DS.

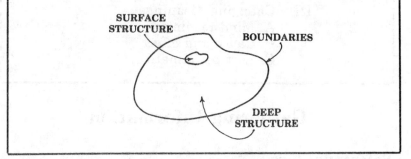

I highly recommend that anyone learning the Meta Model read over this section carefully in order to get the general feel and logic of the model. Then go back to the beginning and start with the first distinction. Attuning yourself to each distinction, hearing it when it comes up, and being able to respond with the appropriate Meta Model response smoothly and naturally usually takes about one week. Then you can easily go on to the next distinction, knowing that the first has become a comfortable, functional habit. Doing this with each distinction will enable you to rapidly and easily incorporate the Meta Model as an exceptionally powerful communication tool.

The Meta Model Outline

This outline is provided as a guide to this section. Notice that there are eight linguistic distinctions in the combined, three major categories. The text will also define several subdistinctions.

   I. Gathering Information
      A. Referential Index
      B. Nominalizations
      C. Unspecified Verbs

  II. Expanding Limits
      A. Modal operators
      B. Universal quantifiers

 III. Changing Meanings
      A. Mind reading
      B. Cause and effect
      C. Lost performative

Gathering Information

Referential Index

In a sentence, the person or thing doing or receiving the action of the verb is called the "referential index." In the Meta Model, these nouns are important because they are SS representations which demonstrate that the speaker has generalized, deleted, or distorted information from his DS.

There are five referential index Meta Model violations. The four which follow include deleted, unspecified, generalized, and reversed referential index. The fifth distinction, nominalizations, forms its own special category.

1. *Deleted referential index* is where the speaker of the sentence simply leaves out the referent. For example, in the sentence, "The window was broken," the agent or actor of the verb "was broken" has been deleted. Of course, there are certain situations where it is obvious that more information is needed. If it were *my* window in the example above, I would immediately ask, "*Who* broke it?!" However, there are many other times when lack of information in a sentence can lead to misunderstanding. The following illustration gives one example of possible consequences of deleting the referent. By the time the young woman provides the missing information, it is already too late.

Deleted Referential Index

When you hear a sentence in which the referent is missing, it is a cue that you need more information. Often, asking for the referent will also assist you in identifying with the speaker specific experiences that may actually be missing from his awareness. This reconnecting with the DS experience not only provides you with the missing information, it can also give the speaker an opportunity to experience a greater sense of awareness and, therefore, more choices about how to feel and behave. Other examples of deleted referential index with an appropriate Meta Model response are:

> Speaker: "I need help."
> Response: "What do you need help with."
>
> Speaker: "I'm being pushed into this mess."
> Response: "Who is pushing you?"
>
> Speaker: "He's not respected."
> Response: "Who doesn't respect him?"

In situations where a person is uncomfortable with the possiblility of being confronted but still wants to express displeasure, this violation is often used. It allows the person to say something which may be controversial or cause conflict, like, "I'm being pushed into this mess," (deleting "by my boss"). Thus, the individual who might respond in an unpleasant way (his boss) has been deleted. This "safe" linguistic pattern is typically used by individuals operating from the auditory and digital representation systems.

2. *Unspecified referential index* occurs when the noun or noun phrase does not name a specific person or thing. Words like "this," "that," "it," or even "thing-a-ma-bob" are all examples of unspecified referential index.

Whenever a person leaves out or does not specify important elements of a sentence, he runs the risk of being misunderstood. The following illustration demonstrates the

Unspecified Referential Index

kind of problems which can arise. In this example, the woman expresses an emotional response to something that does not necesarily relate to the man. She may, for example, be "mad" about a run in her stockings. His response to her original statement, however, indicates that he has chosen to take it personally, setting the stage for what follows. Had the woman been more specific to begin with, the whole scene would have changed dramatically.

Other examples of this Meta Model violation are:

Speaker: "That just won't work."
Response: "What specifically won't work?"

Speaker: "This is important."
Response: "What is important?"

Speaker: "I don't want to talk about it."
Response: "What don't you want to talk about?"

As with the previous Meta Model distinction, Your goal in asking for the missing information is twofold: First, you are asking for information which will help you to better understand the speaker. This can aid in more effective communication. Second, asking for the information which is missing from the speaker's SS is one way of determining whether or not that information is even in the speaker's awareness. For example, if the speaker responded to the first question above with, "I don't know, specifically. It's just a vague sense that things aren't clicking," you immediately know several important things. You know, for example, that the individual is operating from the auditory representational system (see "Predicate Preference" in Chapter II). You also know that the original stimulus for the "vague sense" is outside of his conscious awareness, and, therefore, beyond his control. Discovering this about a speaker can be important in determining just what his model of the world consists of. Reconnecting a speaker with missing DS material by asking the Meta Model Response questions can often provide him with a greater sense of awareness and, thus, more choices about how to feel and behave.

This Meta Model violation is also associated with individuals operating from the auditory and digital representational systems. As with the previous distinction, unspecified referential index is one way to express thoughts and ideas in a way which makes them hard to challenge. By not specifying what they are talking about, "tonals" and "digitals" create a situation in which they are less likely to be contradicted.

It is important to remember that by using the appropriate responses to any of the Meta Model violations, the astute Meta Modeler gains valuable information that can increase his ability to establish rapport. He can also use the patterns to affect, often at a deep unconscious level, the speaker's model of the world. These powerful, positive linguistic interventions operate by expanding both the speaker's perception and his options for responding to the world around him.

3. *Generalized referential index* is one way the speaker can "plug the hole" left by deleting a referent. A generalized referential index is a noun or pronoun which refers to a nonspecific group or category. This violation is common in the English language and is built into popular idioms like "Men don't cry" and "Women are bad drivers." In these two examples, "Men" and "Women" are the generalized referents.

As in the previous distinction, this violation often typifies people who are operating out of the tonal and digital categories. Rather than identify someone specifically who is responsible for an unpleasant situation or experience and risk the possibility of direct confrontation, the speaker simply generalizes the referent into a nonspecific category: *"People who* do those things are not very considerate," or *"One who* becomes upset at a time like this may be considered rather immature." They can even talk about themselves in this indirect manner: "If *one* were to consider such a question...." or "There are *those who* wouldn't agree with you."

This violation can be especially important to catch when the speaker has generalized from one specific person or experience and now includes a whole category from which the original experience is only an example. In Chapter I, for example, Sharon demonstrated as part of her model of the world the generalization: "All *men* are out to take advantage of *women.*" By asking Sharon to specify who she meant by "All men" and "women," the origins of these generalizations could be determined. But more importantly, the process of identifying nonproductive and limiting portions of her model enabled Sharon to again perceive her own power in creating experience for herself. In this distinction, pay attention to pronouns like "they," "everyone," "men," "women," "no one," "people," etc. and to adjectives like "all ___" and "every ___," as well as plural nouns as in "Sports *cars* are dangerous." The illustration below gives one possible outcome of such a statement, innocently spoken but poorly timed.

Generalized Referential Index

Other examples are:

Speaker: "Loving relationships are a drain."
Response: "Which loving relationship(s) do you find draining?"

Speaker: "Now everybody knows."
Response: "Who specifically knows?"

Speaker: "People are so uncaring."
Response: "Who, specifically, is so uncaring?"

82

4. *Reversed referential index* occurs when the speaker is stated as receiving the action of the verb in a sentence rather than doing the action of the verb. You may recognize this pattern as being typical of someone who is depressed. Statements like "Nobody cares about me," and "I sometimes think everyone is out to get me," are examples of this pattern. In both sentences, the speaker has removed himself from a position of being "in charge" of the action and has given the power of acting to someone else. The "me," or speaker, then becomes a helpless victim of whom or whatever is in charge. This is a common pattern used by individuals operating from the kinesthetic system.

The illustration below shows another aspect of this violation. Not only does the man apparently perceive himself as powerless, but he also fails to recognize that he is doing the very thing he is complaining about.

Reversed Referential Index

The famous Gestalt therapist Fritz Perls called this linguistic pattern "projection." As Martin Shepard says in her book *Fritz*, on Page 205, "...whatever we believe about or see in another person or the world at large is invariably a projection. Thus a statement such as 'Nancy is a gossip' was to be rephrased as 'I am a gossip.' " She goes on to say that, as people begin to take responsibility for themselves this way, ". . .they have the possibility of having an 'Aha!' experience, in which there is the recognition 'This is me!' This is referred to as *owning projections.*"

By requiring his clients to reverse positions and become the "active" agent in the sentence, Fritz Perls would put the clients back in charge of the processes of their own existence. This transformed perception of themselves often produced some surprising insights into the model-building behaviors of his clients.

Other examples of this reversal technique are:

> Speaker: "He's no good for me."
> Response: "Try saying, 'I'm no good for him,' and tell me what you experience."

> Speaker: "Everybody hates me."
> Response: "Try saying this: 'I hate everybody.'"

> Speaker: "Nobody loves me."
> Response: "Can you say 'I love nobody?'"

Another form of this violation is often demonstrated by people operating out of the visual communication category. Remember that "visuals" organize experiences in such a way as to prevent "contact" with those around them. One way of maintaining this distance is with the linguistic pattern of reversed referential index. The Meta Model response to these violations will be the same as those above, and you will likely get the same results, the introspective "Aha!"

Examples of this form are:

> Speaker: "He never seems to understand me."
> Response: "I wonder if you would mind saying, 'I never seem to understand him.'"

> Speaker: "She's the one who always seems to get us into these messes.'"
> Response: "Would you mind saying, 'I'm the one who always get us into these messes?'"

Nominalizations

Linguistially, nominalization is the changing of a DS "process" into a SS "event." In other words, it is the changing of a verb which is active in time into a noun which is static or unchanging in time. Since a verb is a process word, it implies active participation by one or more elements. A noun, on the other hand is static and unchanging. It implies no active participation by other elements. Abstract nouns called nominalizations are excellent examples of the process of distortion.

We are taught quite early in our educational experience to form abstract words. Words like "friendship," "sensation," "strategy," etc., assist us in formulating and learning creative and sophisticated concepts. But we are generally not taught to *denominalize* these words. Although the use of these words is important in our complex and technical society, they can also limit a person's sense of control over his life. It is a subtle distinction to make, but the following illustration demonstrates the power these words can have. In this case, the nominalization is the word "decision."

Nominalization

The woman in the above illustration is talking about a "decision" in a special way. She is indicating that she no longer experiences herself in a position to change. She has given up her responsibility to get things done or to even be interested and blames it on something that she is powerless to change. This is much like the example of Sharon in

Chapter I who talked about how her bad "relationships" kept her from getting close to anyone. As with the above illustration, when a person talks about "relationships" in that way, it can indicate a failure to recognize his active participation or responsibility in the continuing process of "relating" with another person.

The illustration below demonstrates how difficult it can be to deal with this linguistic pattern. Without knowledge of the Meta Model response, the woman in the illustration finds herself in just as helpless a position as the man who has nominalized his experience.

Nominalized Individual

When a person systematically uses nominalizations like "love," "fear," or "respect," it may be a good indication that he perceives himself as having few choices and little or no control in his life. The following excerpt is from a highly "nominalized" client. Much like the young man in the illustration above, he is frustrated by the lack of choices he is aware of and by a strong sense that he has lost control over the events of his life.

It's just that this darned *relationship* isn't working out. I mean, every time I turn around, it slaps me in the face. It's like I can't do anything without it being there to remind me of my *obligations,* and you know what a *pain* they

can be! I tell you, I'm just tired of having all
this *responsibility* shoved in my face...

There are two easy ways to determine whether or not a
word is a nominalization. One way is to say the phrase: "An
ongoing _____" in your head, filling in the blank with the
suspected noun. If the phrase makes sense, then it is a
nominalization. Using the first underlined word in the above
excerpt, the phrase "An ongoing *relationship*" makes sense.
The word "relationship" is a nominalization. If we use the
word "desk," as in the phrase "An ongoing *desk*," the phrase
doesn't make sense. The noun "desk" is not a nominalization.

The second way to determine if a noun is a nominalization
involves visualizing a wheelbarrow. It is easy to imagine
placing a noun like "desk," "person," or "apple" into this
imaginary wheelbarrow. These are all *concrete nouns*.
Nominalizations, however, don't "fit" in our imaginary
wheelbarrow. This is because they are distorted forms of
verbs called abstract nouns. From the example above, they
are the words "relationship," "obligations," "pain," and
"responsibility."

When responding to a nominalization, it is important to
assist the speaker in reconnecting with his experience so that
he recognizes the role he plays in the *process* involved. By
changing the noun back into a verb with its actively
participating elements, you assist the speaker in understanding his roll as an active participant. This enables him to
more easily perceive his full range of choices and the control
he can exercise.

In dealing with the "nominalized" client from above, the
following responses could effectively be utilized:

Speaker: "It's just that this darned relationship isn't working out."

Response: "How is the way you are relating
not working out for you?" (Here, the
nominalization is changed back
into a process word, or verb, and is
used to ask for the missing information — see "unspecified verbs.")

Speaker: "...I can't do anything without it being there to remind me of my obligations...."

Response: "To whom are you obligated to do what?"

Speaker: "...you know what a pain they can be."

Response: "How do you experience that pain?" (Here, in order to answer the question, the speaker must change the nominalization back into the process-verb. Again, if his answer does not give you sufficient information, simply ask for the deleted material as demonstrated in the section on unspecified verbs.)

Speaker: "I'm just tired of having responsibility shoved in my face."

Response: "What do you mean 'responsibility?' "

Denominalizing the Medical Model

In an article entitled "Language, Emotion and Disease," Dr. Wallace Ellerbroek[6] makes some astute, if unorthodox, observations. Staff psychiatrist at the Metropolitan State Hospital in Norwalk, California, Dr. Ellerbroek's article addresses the effects of language on our perceptions and behaviors. He contends that, "...each word you use as a label for something makes you see it in an entirely different way." He cites the case of "essential" hypertension, a medical condition for which the cause is unknown. His description includes the process of denominalizing the medical term, a rare action in the field of medicine in which nominalizations abound. Contrary to the generally accepted medical model, he states:

> Remember, I called all diseases "beha-
> viors," in other words, things that
> people do....When I found a patient with
> elevated blood pressure (140/90 mm/Hg
> or more), I said to myself not "He has
> hypertension" but "He is hypertension-
> ing."

This transformation of the nominalization "hypertension," the name given to a specific set of medical conditions, back into a verb or process of "hypertensioning" not only altered Dr. Ellerbroek's perception of his patients but also his behaviors toward them. This, says Dr. Ellerbroek, changed his patients' responses to treatment in a dramatically positive way.

The implication is that as we begin to alter our language, as in the above example, we change our perceptions of the *processes* of health and disease. Ultimately, this gives us more choices about our physical and emotional conditions.

Certain individuals, especially in stressful situations, tend to dissociate from somatic sensations. It is as if they become so uncomfortable physically that they cope by removing from their conscious awareness the source of the unpleasant feelings: their bodies. Though "visuals" tend to dissociate from kinesthetic experience, it is also particularly common of "digitals." They often sound and look very removed from their bodies, their voices and movements so unanimated as to be almost robot-like. This shying away from overly expressive tonality and gestures is similar to the internal experience associated with nominalizations as opposed to the deep structure associated with verb forms. For this reason, "digitals" are said to have "nominalized" their bodies.

Digital Jobs

A person's preferred representational system may influence many aspects of his life, including his choice of careers. It may even be that the language patterns associated with the preferred system are a significant part of the job itself. The following is an example of this generalization.

If you have ever listened to two lawyers arguing a case, you may have noticed some specific linguistic patterns. One very common means of expression is the deletion of themselves (deleted referential index) from the conversations and replacing the "spaces" with

nominalizations. Such phrases as "statistics demonstrate," and "studies have shown," as well as "The situation calls for," and "Under the present circumstances," are combined with an incredible array of legal jargon. This is quite common coming from a person whose preferred representational system is the digital system.

Unspecified Verbs

All verbs are unspecified in that they only symbolize an experience or process; they are not that experience or process. However, for our purposes, there are degrees of specificity within the group of words we call verbs. For example, to say that someone "touched" me is much more generalized than to say that someone "caressed" me. Both verbs imply contact with my person; however, the verb "caressed" is more specific about the kind of contact involved. Another example of the use of unspecified verbs is given in the following scene:

> As I walked up to the young lady on the bench, she wiped a tear from her eye and asked, "Why does my husband always hurt me?"

This is a good example of an often used unspecified verb, "hurt." Again we are faced with the choice of "going inside" and creating the missing information, or we can simply ask

Unspecified Verb

for it. The potential for creating a misrepresentation of the situation is much less likely when we ask for the information. If we try to "make up" the missing material, we might decide, for example, that the young lady was beaten by her husband. Or we might guess that he has been mean to her and she is talking about an emotional "hurt." Either way, we won't know for sure without asking.

The following illustration provides an example of the potential unpleasant effects of such nonspecific communication patterns. In this case, the unspecified verb is "show."

Other examples of this violation and appropriate responses are:

> Speaker: "I feel bad."
> Response: "What are you feeling bad about?"
>
> Speaker: "She is really hard on me."
> Response: "How is she hard on you?"
>
> Speaker: "He could demonstrate some concern."
> Response: "How would you like him to demonstrate concern?"

Sometimes the speaker's response to your request for more information will indicate rules within his model of the world (see "Individual Constraints," Chapter I). In the last example above, the speaker might respond to the question, "How would you like him to demonstrate concern?" with, "He could answer more quickly." This rule, "demonstrating concern = answering quickly" could have special importance in understanding the communication process of this person in certain situations.

This Meta Model violation, unspecified verbs, is particularly common to individuals operating out of the kinesthetic category. They know what they mean by predicates like "hurt," "feels good/bad," "deeply moved," "entangled," etc., and they tend to assume that everyone else knows what they mean. Since this can lead to confusion and misunderstanding, it is often important to challenge this violation.

Since this is a special case of deletion, again your goal is to obtain the information necessary for a complete understanding of the statement as well as discover more about the speaker's model of the world. As you continue to do this, you will begin to discover consistencies in the speaker's model. Attending to these consistencies will assist you in becoming a more effective communicator and will facilitate the entire process of change.

Expanding Limits

The next two distinctions are valuable as a means of assisting in the process of expanding the speaker's model of the world. By gaining more choices about how to feel and think and what to be aware of, the speaker gains more control over how to act and respond in situations which are uncomfortable or painful.

Meta Model Diagram #2

The remaining Meta Model responses involve challenging directly or indirectly limits that are discovered in the speaker's model of the world. These limits are initially presented in the form of the speaker's SS. By using the appropriate Meta Model responses, the boundaries of the DS are defined. Challenging these limits linguistically can assist the speaker in

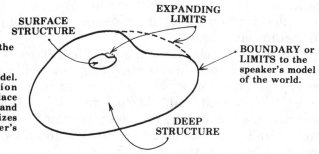

Challenging the boundaries expands the speaker's model. The expansion first takes place with the SS and then generalizes to the speaker's model of the world.

SURFACE STRUCTURE

EXPANDING LIMITS

BOUNDARY or LIMITS to the speaker's model of the world.

DEEP STRUCTURE

---

breaking through confining model limits or restrictions. The results are more choices about how to feel, see and hear the world as well as alternatives to behavior which have been unsatisfactory, painful or limiting.

Modal operators. Modal operator is a linguistic term meaning "modal operator" or "mode of operation." They define the boundaries of the person's model of the world. To extend beyond these boundaries is to invite some *catastrophic expectation* over which the speaker believes he has no control. Bringing this expectation into the conscious awareness of the speaker enables him to test and evaluate its validity. If the limit is found to be unreasonable, the boundaries can be removed from that portion of the speaker's model of the world. This process gives the speaker more choices about his thoughts and feelings. It expands his awareness and allows him to develop alternative behaviors in response to similar situations. The two types of modal operators are described below.

1. *Modal operators of necessity* are exemplified by the imperative "should." For example, someone might say, "I really should be more flexible at times like this." The appropriate Meta Model response is, "What do you think would happen if you weren't more flexible?" This form of question requires that the speaker bring into awareness the underlying catastrophic expectation that elicited the original statement. If he determines that it is valid, that the limit is appropriate and functional, then he can choose to retain it as useful. If, however, it turns out to be a limit which is causing him undue pain or is preventing more appropriate behavior or growth, then it can be explored for its functional elements or discarded in the light of new choices. The illustration below shows both the modal operator of necessity and the catastrophic expectation. The two are often not presented together, and sometimes the speaker is surprised to discover just what his expectation is.

Modal Operator of Necessity

Other words which imply a lack of choice or indicate the speaker's lack of awareness of his participation in and responsibility for his feelings and actions are: "must," "have to," "ought to," and their opposites, "shouldn't," "must not," etc. Examples of this Meta Model violation are:

Speaker: "I must never say those things."
Response: "What will happen if you do?"

Speaker: "I ought to be understanding when he's like that."
Response: "What do you imagine would happen if you weren't?"

Speaker: "I have to believe in it."
Response: "What do you think would happen if you didn't believe in it?"

"Shoulds" are often heard when one person is blaming another: "You should know better than that!" This pattern is typical of someone operating out of the visual model, especially under stress. In this way, a "visual" can verbally externalize his frustration or anger at a person or situation and at the same time exclude himself from having any responsibility for the situation.

2. *A modal operator* of *possibility* is another indication of a potentially counterproductive limitation on a person's model

of the world. When a person says "I can't," he is talking about something he perceives as being outside his ability or sphere of influence. However, it is often simply the person's perception which is limiting, not his ability or the environment or the situation. In the illustration below, for example, the first boy's initial statement followed by his catastrophic expectation is a demonstration of a limit on his model of the world that prevents him from even attempting to get what he wants.

Modal Operator of Possibility

Being presented with a modal operator of possibility can be an excellent opportunity for you to explore with the speaker a limitation or boundary to his model of the world. By responding with the questions, "What stops you?" or "What would happen if you did?," you begin to assist the speaker in determining the validity of the limit and how functional or dysfunctional it is for him. Again, this question brings into awareness the usually unconscious catastrophic expectation in a way it can be dealt with. Other examples from this linguistic pattern are:

> Speaker: "I couldn't say something like that."
> Response: "What would stop you? What would happen if you did?"

> Speaker: "I can't do that."
> Response: "What do you imagine would happen if you did do it?"

Speaker: "It is not possible for me to love anymore."

Response: "What stops you from loving?"

When people who are operating out of the kinesthetic category are under stress, they tend to perceive themselves as having no control, of being "at the mercy" of the situation or of the individuals involved. In this case, it is common for them to use the linguistic form, "I can't...,' because it fits their internal representation of the situation.

The Challenge

Remember, when you begin to challenge a person's model of the world, you may at times shake the very foundations of his belief systems. It is exciting when people begin to understand that they *do* have control in situations where they thought they didn't, and they *can* actually change their thoughts, feelings and behaviors. However, the sudden realization of this additional responsibility may also be uncomfortable or even traumatic to some. Be prepared to provide additional support and understanding to people who begin to make dramatic changes in themselves and their models of reality.

Universal quantifiers. Universal quantifiers are words which imply or state absolute conditions about the speaker's perception of reality. They often indicate that a generalization has been made from a specific experience in the speaker's life. In Chapter I, the case study client, Sharon, expressed during a session that she believed "...all men are out to take advantage of women." She had generalized from several unpleasant experiences that *all* men behaved in a particular way. Linguistically, her use of the word "all," a universal quantifier, indicated that such a generalization had been made. As it was in her case, it can be important to challenge this generalization. This enables a person to discover how his model limits his experience of the world in ways that may be causing undue pain. In the illustration below, the man is so wrapped up in his particular frame of mind that he runs the risk of failing to perceive the happy welcome by his beautiful, healthy family. This is typical of the way universal quantifiers can be indicative of a distorted model of the world.

Universal Quantifier

By helping a speaker to recognize that such a statement is a generalization that is not necessarily based on reality, you begin the process of expanding and changing those perceptions that limit and cause the person to suffer needlessly. The Meta Model response to phrases which include words like "always," "never," "all," "nothing ever," etc. is to ask the speaker if he is aware of any contradictions to his statement. Another effective response is to repeat his statement while exaggerating with your voice the universal quantifiers in order to demonstrate the absurdity or impossibility of the statement. Some examples are:

Speaker: "I never do anything right."
Response: "Can you think of a time when you did something right?"

Speaker: "Everybody's mean to me."

Response: *"Everybody's always* mean to you, *everyone* you know, even your best friend, even the milk man?"

Speaker: "Nothing special ever happens to me."

Response: "I wonder if you can remember at least one time when something special did happen to you."

On the Lighter Side

Humor can have an important place in the therapeutic setting. When the client comes in and is under a great deal of stress and pain, the seriousness of the situation may at times pervade the session. However, humor is an important part of our experience, and when we can laugh at ourselves, it is sometimes easier to accept and change our foibles and failings. The therapist who can utilize humor to lighten, without making light of, the process of change and discovery can often use this talent to quickly gain and maintain positive rapport with his client.

One interesting and useful aspect of universal quantifiers is that they often have built-in, therapeutic, *double binds.*[7] These can be used to assist the speaker in rapidly expanding the implied limit as in the following examples:

Upon hearing the client say, "Though I want to, I'll *never* respect her; I *always* get what I want from her," the therapist responded with: "I have a homework assignment for you. During the coming week I would like for you to ask her to give you only what you want in order to respect her."

When one client entered, saying, "You know, I've *never* learned anything from a therapy session," the counselor responded with: "Well, then, your task for today is to learn one thing for certain, and that is that you can learn nothing from this session."

Changing Meanings

This final section of the Meta Model concerns the logical meanings (semantics) of the words in a person's SS. The following Meta Model violations all have in common the characteristics of either incompleteness or logical impossibility. The words and phrases in this category make up some of the most challenging and useful points from which to embark on the journey into exploring and expanding the speaker's model of the world.

Mind reading. This is the concept that a person can know what other people are feeling or thinking — what their internal experiences are — without verifying it with them.

Mind Reading

This surreptitious presupposition of another's internal state can be the cause of much pain and misunderstanding. As in the above illustration, mind reading can prevent a person from achieving personal goals. This is a case where the phrase, "If only she *really* knew how he feels...," really makes sense!

When someone makes a statement which implies knowledge of another's internal emotional state or thoughts, there are two Meta Model responses you can make. One response can be made only if the person about whom the statement has been made is available. Simply ask the mind reader to check out his statement with that person. If his perception is inaccurate, the other person can assist the speaker in more precisely tuning in to his true thoughts or feelings. Consistently asking individuals in therapy and in other settings to check out their mind reading statements with the people involved sets a good example for more accurate involvement in the process of relating with others.

The other Meta Model response is to simply ask the speaker, "How do you know?" Often his response will give you a surprising amount of information about how he perceives the world around him. You may also get indications of personal rules (see Chapter II) which the speaker utilized in building and maintaining his model of reality. In the above illustration, if the woman were asked how she "knew" that the man "isn't even interested," her response might be "Well, he never seems to look me straight in the eye when we talk. And he doesn't seem to notice when I wear something nice." With this information you now know that for her, looking her straight in the eye and commenting on her clothes means that you are "interested." This can be particularly important information to have in a family setting or in other close relationships. The following excerpt from a family therapy session exemplifies how this linguistic pattern often occurs.

> Jack L., having arrived late to the session, immediately turned to his wife, saying, "I know what you're thinking, all of you! You're disappointed in me. You think I've failed you again. You don't even like me anymore. I'm just a 'bum' to you. Oh, I know you won't admit it, but I can tell."

Somehow, Jack has decided that he already knows what is in each person's head, what their thoughts and feelings are. Having arrived late to the session, these ideas of his are not based on any "concrete" evidence. This is coming from his own expectations, from his own model of the world. This is easily demonstrated by the responses of the other family members to his verbal "outbreak" as he walked into the room. His wife, Joan, speaks first, then their 17-year-old daughter Susan:

> Joan, speaking softly: "Where did that come from? You know Jack, I was just about to tell you how happy I was to see you. I want you to know I'm glad you decided to come (Joan starts to cry), and I don't think you're a bum....I love you."

> Susan: "Me too, daddy. What makes you think we're disappointed in you? I'm just glad you're here."

The therapist next asked, "Jack, what was it that led you to think that everyone was disappointed in you, that they didn't like you and thought you were a bum?" Jack's response tells us a great deal about his model of the world, including some of his own personal rules.

> "Well, I don't know. When I walked in, I saw that everyone was sitting with their arms folded, you know, like they were all mad or something. When I went to sit down by my wife, she wouldn't look at me, she just kept staring at the floor, you know, like people do when they're pissed off. I know that look! Susie, there, she just frowned at me, like I was some kind of bum, you know, some stranger. I've done a lot of things I shouldn't have; it would serve me right if nobody liked me!"

Calibrated Communication

Mind reading plays a special part in *calibrated communication* or *calibrated loops.* These are unconscious, often pain-producing patterns of communication that can be observed between individuals in couples and in families.[8] The excerpt from the session with Jack and his family revealed that Jack's wife's staring at the floor meant something specific to Jack. His "I know that look" indicated at least a partial awareness on his part of a familiar pattern of communication between them. This "loop," the sequence of "the look" and his response to it, was repeated several times during the session. Whenever Jack's wife stared at the floor, he became sullen and uncomfortable. His response was not related to the content of the ongoing conversation but was based on minor *subliminal cues.* These are unconscious non-verbal communications that have special meanings to the individuals involved. These special meanings are often an important part of an individual's complex equivalents (see Chapter I). In Jack's case, looking at the floor = "being pissed off." As a therapist or counselor or any person who works with people, your ability to recognize and bring these patterns into the awareness of those involved can help disarm their harmful effects.

Mind reading is insidious in that it can work two ways. One way, demonstrated in the previous examples, comes out as "I know what you're thinking." The other form of mind reading occurs when a person believes that others should know what *he* is thinking or feeling. The illustration below is an example of this form of reversed or *projected mind reading.*

When this pattern is used, the speaker reverses the mind reading and projects it onto others. The woman in the illustration, for example, believes that since she "knows" without asking what makes the man happy, then he "should know" without asking what makes her happy. Challenging

Projected Mind Reading

this form of mind reading is just as important as challenging the other form. Some examples of the mind reading distinctions are:

Speaker: "I know what's good for him."
Response: "How do you know what is good for him?"

Speaker: "I can tell she doesn't like me."
Response: "How can you tell she doesn't like you?"

Speaker: "He should know better."
Response: "How should he know not to do that?"

Speaker: "If she really cared about me, she wouldn't have to ask what I need."
Response: "If she doesn't ask, then how will she know for sure what you need?"

The mind reading pattern is often associated with people operating out of the visual communication category. It can come out in an accusing "I know what you're thinking!" or in the more direct "You ought to know better than that!" This linguistic form implies a need in the speaker to be in control of the environment through omniscient "knowing" and is often communicated with the "I shouldn't have to tell you" format.

Cause and effect. Cause and effect is a particularly widespread and potentially pain-producing Meta Model violation. It is the belief that an action such as a verbal or facial expression can *cause* another person to experience a definite emotion or "inner state." The person responding believes he has no choice in how to respond. A statement like, "You make me mad," implies that there is no other possible way to respond. It is as if the speaker has relinquished all responsibility for creating his own emotional state. The fallacy of the cause and effect presuppositions becomes apparent when some action by one person results in completely different responses from others involved, as in the illustration below.

Cause and Effect: Different Responses

There are two ways in which cause and effect belief systems can bring about pain or unhappiness. First, the belief that someone else can create in you an emotional state implies that you have no control over your own feelings or thoughts. Without this control, not only are you unable to change your inner experience in order to become more comfortable, but you are also dependent on others to create "good" feelings inside of you.

Second, since you believe that you can cause another person to experience pleasurable emotions, then you can also cause them to experience pain and sorrow. With this "power" comes a sense of responsibility as the "causal agent." When you "make" someone sad, then you feel guilty and often want to know if there is "anything I can do" to "make them feel better." Within this belief system, it is possible to persecute yourself for something that you actually have no control over, since you cannot cause or create a different outcome. The effects of this pattern are illustrated below. The man finds himself in a quandry as a result of his cause and effect belief system. Questioning these quasi-causal connections can often assist a person in experiencing more choices and much less pain and guilt in his life.

Cause and Effect

As the instructor of a seminar on the Meta Model I was once questioned by a young woman who firmly believed that the feelings and emotions of a client are very much in the hands of the therapist. She stated her belief that a therapist has a "duty and responsibility to ensure that a client doesn't 'feel bad'." Though I agreed that "irresponsible behavior" on the part of any people helper is unethical, I maintained the premise that one person cannot take the responsibility as the *causal agent* for another's emotions. The following transcript from that seminar gives one possible response to this cause and effect belief system.

B.L.: "Then you're saying that it isn't right to go around 'pushing other people's buttons'."

Woman: "Not if it might make them feel bad. You have an obligation, especially with clients, to say things in a way that will make them feel better.'

B.L.: "You mean, then, that it is important to push the 'good-feelings' buttons?"

Woman: "Yes, exactly. As a therapist you're in a position to selectively push the buttons that will make the client feel better."

B.L.: "What you're saying, then, is that, if you were my client, it would be possible for me to push your buttons. Please tell me quickly, are they on the front of you or on your back? I wouldn't want to push a wrong one by accident!"

After the laughter died down — the woman laughed good-naturedly, too — I continued, saying, "Seriously, I think it's important for each of you to decide for yourself just where those "buttons" are and whether you believe they are on the inside or on the outside. If they're on the outside, seek professional help immediately! If they're on the inside,

well, then, thank goodness. At least
you know who pushes them now,
don't you?!

By challenging this belief system when it is being counter-
productive or causing undue pain, you can assist the speaker
in having more choices about how to feel and operate in the
world. There are two ways to challenge this violation. Ask
the speaker to tell you how, specifically, he caused the other
person to feel that way. Or ask how the other person makes
the speaker feel a particular way. This will give you a great
deal of information about how the speaker makes sense of
the world and how he perceives himself in relation to others.
This information may be invaluable in the ongoing processes of positive change and growth.

This pattern is typical of the person acting from the
kinesthetic communication category. Generally, it comes out
as "You hurt me when you say those things (I have no
control over my feelings)," or "I'm sorry if I've hurt your
feelings (I don't deserve this power over you; I feel guilty for
using it)." Some examples and Meta Modal responses are:

Speaker: "Their laughter makes me mad."
Response: "How does their laughing cause you
            to be mad?"

Speaker: "She upsets me."
Response: "What, specifically, does she do
            that you feel upset about?"

Speaker: "I feel bad for making her cry."
Response: "What did you do that you believe
            made her cry?"

Choices

It is not always necessary to challenge
directly the cause and effect belief system in
the therapeutic setting. When people present
this pattern in their SS, it is sometimes more

important to bring into their conscious awareness the specific behaviors which they believe
to be the cause of the emotional states. By
maintaining a *meta perspective* — an awareness of the *pattern* involved — you can effectively lead the speakers to an understanding of
the concept in ways that are more relevant to
them personally. In this way you would not
deal directly with the more abstract ideology
that underlies their belief system but would
concentrate on more pragmatic, practical
implications of the pattern.

One mistaken notion sometimes arises during the teaching
of the concept of cause and effect to groups. Some people
think it implies that a person may do whatever he likes
regardless of others. I would like to stress that a person who
is behaving in a responsible manner is cognizant enough of
others to take into account how they *may choose* to respond
to his behaviors. Most individuals do not care to spend time
with someone who behaves in a way which is unpleasant to
them. People learn early what kinds of behavior will get
them what they want, and these are incorporated into their
models of the world. Everyone is always acting in accord-
ance with these models.

Lost performative. Lost performative refers to judg-
ments, beliefs, or standards expressed by a person in such a
way that the individual who is making the judgment or
setting the standard is not identified in the speaker's SS.
These statements usually come out as generalizations about
the world, and they have no apparent connection with the
speaker. In the illustration below, it is hard to tell whether
the girl is simply "parroting" something she has heard or
actually believes what she is saying. Of course, the boy's
response to her initial statement indicates what he thinks
about the matter!

Lost Performative

Only too often, these generalized statements about the world come from the speaker's own model. By linguistically leaving himself out as the evaluator or judge, the speaker indicates the possibility that there are limits within his model that he doesn't recognize as being self-imposed. By requesting the speaker to identify the "judge" who is making these value judgements, you can assist him in confronting those limits or rules in his model of the world. Once they have been identified, they can be challenged for their validity, especially if they are preventing the speaker from experiencing a fuller, richer life.

Some examples of this violation that are often indicative of unconscious, limiting rules are:

Speaker: "That's a stupid thing to do."
Response: "That's stupid according to whom?"

Speaker: "Oh, it's not important anyway."
Response: "It's not important to whom?"

Speaker: "It's not good to be strict."
Response: "Not good to whom?"

By getting the speaker to use such phrases as "*I* think..." or "*My* belief is...," the speaker is able to identify himself as the specific performer of the judgment, thought, belief or action.

Without that identification, any challenge to the belief system is irrelevant.

In keeping with their tendency to be "nominalized," removing themselves from any position which might leave them open to criticism or challenge, "tonals" and "digitals" both commonly use this pattern. It is possible to make sweeping generalizations, profound truths and important judgements and not ever identify yourself as the originator of such. An example of this pattern is: "Statistically speaking, results demonstrate that under prime conditions it is considered in the *best* interests of all concerned that it is *important* to be assertive."

Summary

The Meta Model Reframed

Now that you have learned the Meta Model, here is a brief summary of the model in terms of seven basic Meta Model response questions.

Gathering Information

1. *Who, what, where, when, how, specifically?*
   Use: When information is left out of the speaker's SS (deleted) or when it has been unspecified or generalized.
   Example: When speaker says, "I'm depressed," ask, "What is depressing you; what are you depressed about?"
   Example: When speaker says, "Everyone's against me," ask "Who specifically is against you?"

2. *Can you say that about yourself?*
   Use: When the speaker says something about another person that may apply to himself.

Example: When the speaker says: "She never seems to understand me," say, "Can you say "I never seem to understand her?"

Example: When the speaker says "My boss hates me," say, "What do you experience when you say, 'I hate my boss'?"

Expanding Limits

3. *What stops you? What would happen if you did?* (catastrophic expectations)

Use: When you hear words like "can't" or "should."

Example: When speaker says, "I can't love," ask, "What stops you from loving?"

Example: When speaker says, "I must be understanding," ask, "What would happen if you weren't?"

4. *Can you think of a time (situation) when you did (didn't)?"*

Use: When the speaker indicates the belief that there are *no* exceptions.

Example: When speaker says, "Everyone thinks I'm stupid," ask, "Can you tell me one person who doesn't? You mean *everyone* thinks you're stupid, even your pet rock?"

Example: When speaker says, "I'm always late," ask, "Can you think of a time when you weren't late?"

Changing Meanings

5. *How do you know?*

Use: When the speaker is mind reading.

Example: When speaker says, "I know he doesn't love me," ask, "How do you know?"

Example: When speaker says, "He should know better," ask, "How should he know?"

6. *How do they (you) make you (them) feel that way?*
Use: When the speaker expresses cause — effect relationships with others' emotions.
Example: When speaker says, "She makes me angry," ask, "How does she make you angry?"
Example: When speaker says, "I feel bad for making her unhappy," ask, "What did you do that you believe made her unhappy?"

7. *According to whom?*
Use: When you hear an unsubstantiated value judgement.
Example: When speaker says, "That was a stupid thing to do," ask, "Stupid according to whom?"
Example: When speaker says, "His incompetence bothers me," ask, "Who believes that he is incompetent?"

CHAPTER IV:

THE VISUAL MODEL

The youth searched for the answer in the
direction first indicated by the old man. But
nothing was there. And when she returned her
gaze back to his face, she realized that he had
not directed her attention out over the land-
scape, but rather inward into the vast reaches
of her being.

Pupil Response

In the early 1960's there appeared on the market a unique
type of sun glasses. They were very much like a one-way
mirror: the wearer could comfortably see out, much like
ordinary shaded glasses, but no one could see in through
their mirror-like reflection. They quickly gained in popular-
ity and soon were given the colloquial name "cheaters."

The significance of that name lies in the profound intuitive
awareness we have of the importance of our eyes in
communication. Some people are more alert than others to
what is communicated by the eyes. In his discusssion of
Middle Eastern cultures, Hall states that the Arabs have
known about *pupil response* for years. This unconcious

113

response is an "emotional indicator." Says Hall, "Since people can't control the response of their eyes, which is a dead giveaway, many Arabs...wear dark glasses, even indoors."[1]

Desmond Morris also addresses this phenomena in his book *Manwatching,* saying, "...the jade dealers of pre-Revolutionary China...took to wearing dark glasses expressly in order to hide their excited pupil dilations when they were handed a particularly valuable specimen of jade."[2] Especially important in Western cultures where the "look-to-listen" rule is so widespread, our eyes play a critical part in communicative processes.

The Visual System

This diagram of the visual system shows how visual input is transmitted by the optic nerve to the brain. Notice how input from the right and left fields of vision go to opposite sides of the brain. This crossover occurs at a junction called the Optic chiasma.

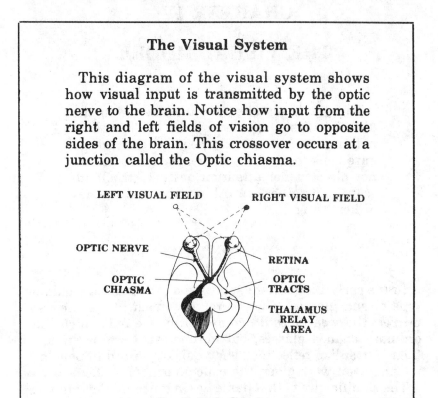

Occipital Cortex

Visual sensations may be generated by stimulation other than light, such as pressure on the eyeball and electric stimulation of certain parts of the brain.

It is the sympathetic division of the Autonomic Nervous System (ANS) which acts to change pupil size in response to emotional stimulation. Even conditions of mild arousal or interest will systematically affect the pupil. Knowing what emotional states elicit these systematic changes can give the astute observer a special kind of "insight" into a person's internal state.

Eckhard Hess began to study pupil dilations as a psychologist at the University of Chicago. His research stimulated a great deal of interest in "expressive eyes,"[3] showing that pupil dilation or constriction is an extremely accurate indicator of that person's response to stimulation. Results demonstrated that when a person is interested or aroused, the pupil dilates. When confronted with unpleasant or noxious stimuli, the pupil constricts.

Ocular Accessing Cues

When someone is trying to "remember" something, part of what you see, if you watch closely, are specific patterns of movement and changes in the person's physiology related to the process of remembering. As you read the following examples, imagine that you are closely watching the people described.

Rita told us that she was confused. She sat for a long moment with her head bowed, and she shook it slowly from side to side. Finally, gazing down at the floor to her left, she muttered, "Somehow, it just doesn't feel right."

From Rita's words, you can easily guess that she is very much into her feelings. However, there is another piece of important information given by *just her eyes alone.*

As if the ceiling behind me could somehow give
him the answer, he searched intently back and
forth over my brow, saying, "Let me see now."

This person's words provide one immediate clue: he is
somehow visually "searching" for information. And again
we are presented with analog gesturing just as informative
as the words: what he is doing with his eyes.

In the mid-1970's Bandler and Grinder began to study the
patterns of movements of people's eyes as people thought
and spoke. They discovered that these movements correlated
fairly well with certain types of information retrieval
behaviors. These systematic patterns of behavior were
eventually formalized into a model called *accessing cues*.

Eye-Scanning Patterns

When people are thinking and talking, they move their
eyes in what is known as *eye-scanning patterns*. These
movements appear to be symptomatic of their attempts to
gain access to internally stored or internally generated
information. This information is encoded in our minds in one
or more of the representational systems (see Chapter II).
When a person "goes inside" to retrieve a memory or to
create a new thought, he exhibits certain behaviors indicative of the representational system he is accessing at the
moment. The two examples given above demonstrate these
accessing behaviors in action.

Split-Brain Theory: Two-in-One

"Split-brain studies at the California Institute
of Technology during the 50's and 60's opened
up a whole new field of brain research. Under
the direction of Roger Sperry, a Cal Tech group
conducted research on patients whose epileptic
seizures had been controlled by an operation
which severed the corpus callosum and related
cummissures. This procedure isolated one

cerebral hemisphere from the other by severing the communication pathways between them.[5]

Major results of the research indicated a *hemispheric specialization*. Each hemisphere of the brain apparently employs different modes of processing information (see diagram below). It is possible that this specialization of brain function is being emulated by a person's eye-scanning movements when he is thinking and calling upon different portions of the brain to process information.

The following list of words from J. E. Bogen[6] indicates parallel ways of "knowing." The drawing represents the two hemispheres of the brain and the bilateral crossover which is most obvious as "handedness." A right-handed person has a dominant left-hemisphere; a left-handed person has a dominant right-hemisphere.

LEFT HEMISPHERE	RIGHT HEMISPHERE
intellect	intuition
convergent	divergent
digital	analogic
secondary	primary
abstract	concrete
directed	free
propositional	imaginative
analytic	holistic
linear	nonlinear
rational	intuitive
sequential	multiple
objective	subjective
successive	simultaneous

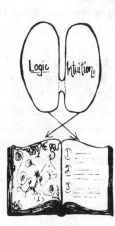

Eye-scanning patterns are the most easily observable accessing behavior. Descriptions which follow are based on patterns usually exhibited by right-handed people (left hemisphere dominant). The patterns are reversed for *some* left-handed individuals. Please notice that this is another generalized model. It is advisable when possible to check out your observations by either direct questioning or by correlating eye patterns with other accessing behaviors. See also the section on "Mapping" in this chapter.

When you observe people talking or thinking, you may notice their eyes constantly in motion, darting back and forth, up and down, occasionally glancing at objects and people but just as often "focused" on inner experiences. As previously mentioned, these movements are symptomatic of the way they are thinking. In the descriptions that follow, the word "looking" refers to the movement of a person's eyes in the direction indicated. "Left" means towards *that* person's left, and "right" means towards *his* right. It is helpful to keep in mind that this accessing behavior represents "looking" internally. That is, during the moment of information retrieval, people are generally *not* conscious of external visual stimuli. Rather, they are concentrating on internally stored or internally generated images, sounds, words, and feelings. Please notice also that the italicized words below indicate the kind of information being accessed.

> **Looking up and to the right:** *Constructed images.* These are visual images or pictures which are created by the individual. They can be recombinations of pieces of previously experienced visual input (see "eidetic images") into new or novel forms or sequences, or they can be created images which are constructed in response to other sensory stimuli. Constructed images are usually characterized by flatness or lack of depth and sometimes by a lack of color.

> **Looking up and to the left:** *Eidetic images.* These are stored visual images or pictures of past events and other previously experienced

visual stimuli. This includes dreams and constructed images that have already been experienced. These images are usually characterized by having both depth and motion — as in a movie — as well as color.

Looking level and to the right: *Constructed speech.* This pattern is usually associated with the process of creating spoken language. In this position, the person is "putting into words" what he wants to say next.

Looking level and to the left: *Remembered sound.* This includes such tonal representation as the "alphabet tune" and letters, advertisement jingles, phone numbers, and colloquialisms like slang and swearing. This is also where a person often moves the eyes when remembering *auditory tape loops:* messages stored in short, often tuneful or rhythmic patterns which have been so often repeated that the person has lost conscious awareness of their existence. One example of this is the "Remember-to-get-the-milk-on-the-way-home-from-work" line that is recited so often during the course of the morning that it eventually drops from conscious awareness.

Note: The next two eye-scanning patterns are often reversed in both right and left-handed people. It is important to determine which pattern is being used by an individual (see "Mapping") before you can use the information gained from observing these eye movements.

Looking down and to the right: *Feelings.* In this position a person can access both derived feelings (emotions) and stored kinesthetic memories. Think of the position you often see a depressed person in: head bowed, shoulders rounded, body drawn into itself. That person is really "into his feelings." Remember that for some individuals, accessing feelings will be down and to the left.

Looking down and to the left: *Internal dialog.*[7] Usually associated with "deep thought," these are the words and sounds made internally that accompany this process. (At times these sounds and exclamations may "leak" out without a person's being aware of it: "Please stop mumbling to yourself" is an often heard response to this leakage.) Typically, internal dialog is a running commentary on your current experience. At quieter moments, it can be an analytic tool of complex, rational, logical thinking. (This would be "rational" and "logical" only relative to the individual's model of reality, not necessarily to a general consensus of reality!) This accessing pattern may be down and to the right for some individuals.

Defocused Eyes: *Visualization.* This may be in any of the above positions and is very often used during face-to-face conversations by individuals who communicate using the "look to listen" rule. This is usually accessing of either eidetic or constructed visual imagery. However, it may also indicate accessing of other forms of information. When in doubt, check it out!

Closed Eyes: *Taste and smell.* Although people often close their eyes in order to remember a particular taste or smell, watch for movements of the eyes under the lids. These movements can indicate any of the previously discussed accessing cues and can be interpreted as if the eyes were open. The following illustratations demonstrate how the eye positions appear to the observer. Put together, they form the *accessing cues schematic.*

LOOKING UP AND TO THE RIGHT:
constructing images

LOOKING UP AND TO THE LEFT:
remembering images

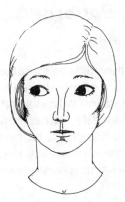

LOOKING LEVEL AND TO THE RIGHT:
constructing speech

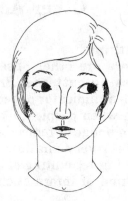

LOOKING LEVEL AND TO THE LEFT:
remembering sounds

| LOOKING DOWN AND TO THE RIGHT: *feelings* | LOOKING DOWN AND TO THE LEFT: *internal dialog* |

NOTE: This schematic is reversed for some left-handed people.

CAUTION: This represents a *generalization* of human behavior.

REMEMBER: **When in doubt, check it out!**

Other Accessing Patterns

Breathing

There are other observable behaviors associated with accessing patterns. *Breathing,* for example, can be an excellent indicator of certain information retrieval patterns. Often when people are accessing visually, either constructing an image or remembering eidetic images, their breathing becomes very shallow. It can even stop altogether! The following recounting of a therapy session demonstrates how this kind of information can be useful.

> The therapist has noticed that when the husband (Joe) faces his wife, there are often long pauses in his breathing. At particularly stressful times he even holds his breath. Joe

has just indicated that whenever his wife looks at him "a particular way," he feels upset (see "complex equivalents," page 27).

Therapist: "Would you tell me, Joe, how your wife's looking at you that way causes you to be upset?"[8]

Joe's immediate nonverbal response to the question is to glance up and to his left. As he does so, his breathing almost stops, and there is a long pause before he speaks. This matches the behavior previously observed by the therapist. Joe: "I don't know. I just get the idea she's disgusted or angry with me or something."

From Joe's analog response, the therapist has a very important and potentially useful piece of information. His behavior indicates a strong possibility that Joe is "seeing" an internal image from some past experience (an eidetic image). When Joe "sees" this image, he becomes upset. It is important to note that Joe is completely unaware of this process ("I don't know. I just get the idea....")

If this is true, then it is not actually his wife's looking at him that "certain way" that is upsetting him. It is, rather, some visually coded memory that is elicited or brought to mind by that look. In effect, Joe is responding to an *internally generated* experience (see pages 24 — 25) rather than to the externally presented stimuli. After determining from Joe that his wife is still looking at him "that way," the therapist's intervention demonstrates how a slight change in Joe's behavior can have a dramatic effect on his experience.

Therapist: "Joe, I wonder if you could look at

your wife again, and as you do, I would like you to do two things: I want you to continue to look at her rather than looking away, and, as you look at her I want you to take several slow deep breaths. Will you do that?"

Joe: "Uh, sure, I guess so." As he carries out the therapist's instructions, Joe experiences a moment of confusion, but as it passes, he comments: "Say, you know I didn't feel that way this time!"

A portion of the remaining session was devoted to instructing Joe on how and when he could use this "new behavior" to help him achieve his goal of "better communication" with his wife.

Body Posture

Body posture can also be a good indicator of how a person is accessing information. It is much easier to "visualize" when you assume a "visual's" posture: back staight and erect, chin raised and forward, eyes looking up, and breathing shallow. To access feelings, round the shoulders and back, lean forward, and breathe deeper into the abdomen. Taking the "telephone" posture with the head tilted to one side we can facilitate tonal information accessing, while the arms-folded, head back posture of the "digital" is a good way to become digitalized.

Minimal Cues

Often people will exhibit very slight shifts or variations from their "normal" stature. These behaviors are *minimal cues.* By training yourself to be alert to these slight shifts, you can often catch subtle nuances of communication that pass most people by at the conscious level.

Auditory accessing is often simply a slight tilt of the head as the person recalls "tape loops" or tries to remember what someone has said. Deep thought utilizing internal dialog looks much like Rodin's famous sculpture of "The Thinker," with various personal modifications. A slight stiffening of the spine or tensing of the shoulders can indicate visual processing, while the opposite minimal cues — rounded shoulders and curved spine — can indicate that a person is "getting in touch" with the information.

Going Through the Motions

Have you ever walked into a room and then, having forgotten what it was that you were after, found yourself retracing your steps in order to remember? What you are doing is literally placing your body back into physical positions which will help you remember. (Of course, visual and other cues along the way also help.) Often, in order to accurately describe a particular, complex motion like a golf swing or tennis serve, the person giving the description will find himself literally going through the motions. These are both examples of a special case of kinesthetic accessing involving movement. As you become more alert to minimal cues people give as they communicate, you will notice people's muscles involuntarily responding with subtle movements as they recall the gross motor movements of the actions they are accessing.

Mapping

Mapping is a process by which you can determine both an individual's preferred representational system and also that person's eye-scanning accessing patterns. For example, with Part A that follows, you can determine whether a person systematically looks down left for feelings or for internal dialog. Since accessing cues may be reversed in some left-handers, it can be important to determine which side of the visual eye-scanning pattern is eidetic imaging and which is constructed imaging. Once you know this information, you will find that it remains fairly constant for any individual. Though accessing patterns seem to remain stable in adults, children below the age of six or seven do not demonstrate patterns as consistent as children who are older. This may occur due to the development of hemispheric dominance which theoretically doesn't develop before that age.

Part B of the mapping process demonstrates how a person is responding to the environment at that particular moment and may also indicate habitual patterns of information accessing. With this information, you can discern a person's preferred representational system and representational system hierarchy. Remember, however, that these can change depending on such variables as setting, amount of stress the individual is experiencing, and his or her internal response to you.

Mapping may be used to simply verify the meaning of one small piece of behavior or information. In the example where Joe exhibited the analog behavior of glancing up and to the left, the therapist could verify that he was "seeing" an eiditic image by simply asking the appropriate mapping question. Or you can map a person completely prior to a formal counseling session. Mapping can be done overtly, or the questions can be embedded in the course of an ordinary interview. Eventually, as you "tune" yourself to the people around you, you may find that the process of mapping people becomes an automatic part of your own communicative behavior. Done in this way, almost unconsciously, it can be a tremendously useful means of both gathering important information and gaining rapport.

Part A: Mapping the
Accessing Cue Schematic

As you ask the questions which follow, pay attention to the person's eyes as well as to shifts in posture and breathing. Sometimes the response is so minimal it is hard to detect. If you fail to get a satisfactory response, go on to the next question and come back to it later. The questions given here are only examples. You can be creative and generate questions of your own, but pay attention to the predicates you use. If they presuppose a representational system which is different from the one you are testing, the person may be led into the accessing pattern associated with that system.

1. **Constructed images.** Ask a visual question about the future, like, "What do you imagine (I, this town, that tree) will look like ten years from now?" This requires the person to construct an image of something he has not yet experienced.

2. **Eidetic images.** Ask a visual question about the past like, "What color was your first car?" or about specific information like, "How many windows are there on the front of your house?" This calls to mind some previously experienced image.

3. **Constructed speech.** Ask for a complex verbal response like, "What does it mean to be 'predisposed'?" If you preface this question with the directions, "Just think about what you would say without answering," you allow for the "rehearsal" of speech.

4. **Remembered sounds.** Ask for auditory recall from the recent past or from a well-rehearsed "tape loop" like, "What was the first question I asked you?" or "What letter comes before 'p' in the alphabet?"

5. **Feelings.** Ask a question which presupposes the kinesthetic system, especially derived feelings like, "How did you feel on the day before your last birthday?" or "What was the most (exciting, scary, happy) experience you have ever had?" Again, asking the person to simply think of the experience without verbally responding may give you a better analog response.

6. **Internal dialog.** Often the most difficult to
detect, this cue is best observed as it naturally
occurs, usually when a person is not being
required to interact with others. Sometimes this
cue can be elicited by asking questions such as,
"During the quieter moments in your life, what
do you find yourself thinking about?"

It is important to note that people will often *lead* with the
accessing pattern which is most comfortable to them. A
"visual," for example, may first access with a visual
accessing pattern when asked to say what letter comes
before the letter "p" in the alphabet. What he is doing is
using a visual *lead system* to create an image of the alphabet
in order to answer the question. When a person persists in
using one of the accessing patterns as the initial step in
gaining the information, it may take several questions of the
same type before you can observe the accessing cue for which
you are testing.

One thing which can assist you in eliciting the pattern you
are testing for is to *model* the posture, tonality, and other
minimal cues which match the communication category and
representational system presupposed by the question you are
asking. For example, when asking a kinesthetic question,
rounding your shoulders slightly, bending forward, speaking
somewhat lower, and using a "placating" palm-up hand
gesture may help direct the person's attention at an
unconscious level to that accessing pattern.

Part B: Mapping the
Preferred System and Hierarchy

In the following sections you will again be watching for
accessing cues — eye movements, shifts in breathing and
posture, and other indications of systematic use of information retrievel behaviors. Since it is important in the sections
which follow to know what a person's typical accessing
patterns are — whether down left or down right for feelings,
for example — it is necessary to have already mapped the
person's accessing cues schematic (see Part A). As you
observe how a person responds in each of the sections below,

you will be able to identify both his preferred representational system and his representational system hierarchy. As in Part A, the wording of the instructions given are only representative of what could be said. Use your own ideas in creating the instructions and questions that will be most compatible with your normal way of communicating.

Section I. Give these instructions before proceeding with the three steps below: "I'm going to say a few words, and I want you to listen to them, think about them, and be sure that you know what they mean. You don't have to tell me anything. Just listen and understand. Are you ready?"

1. *Concrete noun.* Say a concrete noun like "dog," "tree," or "boat," then pause and observe the nonverbal response as the person hears and makes sense of what he has heard. These responses will be so fast and subtle that it will require your utmost attention.

What you are watching for is an accessing pattern. For example, upon hearing the word "dog," a "kino" might look down and to the right as he accesses the *feelings* associated with his *understanding* of what the word "dog" represents to him. A "visual" might glance up and to the left, creating an *image* of a dog associated with his *understanding,* while a "tonal" or "digital" may glance from one side to the other, repeating the word "dog" and associating it with other auditory elements. Watch for *consistent* use of one of these patterns as you continue below.

2. *Abstract noun.* Say an abstract noun — a nominalization — like "friendship" or "manifestation," then wait for the nonverbal response. The reponses will usually be almost immediate.

3. *Nonsense syllables.* Say a nonsense word

like, "termonacar" or "frucerah" (be inventive), then pause and wait for the response. This technique is particularly effective because in order to make sense of what he has heard, the person must draw upon information from his own model of the world. You have disrupted his expectations by saying a word that doesn't make sense, and the confusion that results from the surprise nonsense syllables creates a mildly stressful situation in which he will most likely retreat to his preferred system in order to make sense of what he has just experienced.

Section II. Give these instructions prior to the next two steps: "I'm going to ask you to think about some things you may have experienced or you might experience, but I won't ask you to describe them to me. Just think about them. Ready?"

1. *Past event.* "Can you remember your last (birthday, vacation, fun weekend)?" By asking the person to draw on his experience in a general way using the unspecified verb, "remember", you allow him to recall the experience in the way that is most comfortable to him, usually his preferred representational system. Again, allow time for the person to fully respond before going on the next question.

2. *Future event.* "Where do you think you will be living ten years from now?" Notice the use of the nonsensory-specific word "think." Observe which system the person uses in order to create the response to this question.

Section III. This final section requires some spontaneity on your part as well as attention to what you *do* and to what you *say:* they will be different! Your goal will be to determine which of two simultaneously presented, *incongruent* (different) *messages* is received by the person you are working with. This will give you the person's representational system hierarchy. Study these examples closely and practice them before trying them out. Notice that each step has two parts, "Say" and "Do," which *overlap* as indicated.

1. *Auditory/Visual incongruence.*

Say: "I'm going to ask you to pay attention to your internal experience while we do (see *Do* below) two things."

Do: As you say the word "two" above, hold up *three* fingers for just a moment, then put them down. Do this casually, and after a few moments, ask the person, "What was the first thing you were aware of as I spoke a moment ago?"

The person's response to the question will indicate whether he was more alert to the auditory portion of the experience or to the visual portion. If he points out the incongruity between what you said and what you did, he scores visual over auditory.

2. *Kinesthetic/Auditory incongruence.*

Say: "Pay attention to your thoughts as I touch you on your right (see *Do* below) knee."

Do: As you say the word "right" above, reach out and gently touch the person on his *left* knee. This is especially effective if you maintain the person's visual contact with your face, rather than with your hand. Do this by watching the person's face as you are speaking and reaching over to touch his knee. When you are through, ask, "What were you aware of as I touched you a moment ago?" If the person detects the incongruity, he scores kinesthetic over auditory.

2. *Visual/Kinesthetic incongruence.*

Say: "Tell me what you are aware of as I do
this (see *Do* below).

Do: As you say the word "this," with one
hand gently touch the person, while with
the other hand "scribe an arc" across the
person's field of vision.

Again, this will indicate where the person's
attention is drawn. The person's response will
let you know how to score.

Of course, this heirarchy testing leaves out the digital
representational system. A "digital" will be more likely to
score auditory and visual over kinesthetic. However, a
"digital" will also tend to score visual over auditory, while an
"auditory" will tend to score auditory over visual. In any
event, it is important to take into consideration all aspects of
a person's communicative output. The mapping skills
described above are only one of the ways to facilitate
understanding and determine which system of communication to use in order to obtain the rapport and trust necessary
for influential communication. For more on identifying a
person's hierarchy, see Appendix B.

Summary

The Visual Model provides us with a format for seeing,
understanding and utilizing consistent patterns of observable behavior. Based in part on research and pragmatic
applications of the Bandler-Grinder model, these techniques
provide quick and efficient means for determining the
representational system being used by an individual at any
particular moment.

Pupil response is a very accurate indicator of interest or
arousal. With good light, pupil response can be seen from as
far away as five feet or more. Close observation of a person's
eyes during the uttering of key words or phrases can assist
you in determining his areas of concern and interest. As both
the jade dealers and the Arabs have realized, this response

cannot be controlled, since it is governed by the sympathetic nervous system.

Eye-scanning patterns or accessing cues also provide information about how an individual is thinking. Combined with breathing and postural shifts, they can prove to be extremely useful in assisting people to discover and change limiting and pain-producing behaviors. As in the example where Joe creates uncomfortable feelings from an unconscious eidetic image (see page 123) these behaviors usually operate outside a person's awareness and control.

The mapping process can assist you in determining the meaning of certain patterns of behavior. Part A is designed to help you identify the specific eye motion associated with each type of thinking. Sections 1 and 2 of Part B give you information about what representational system(s) a person habitually uses (the preferred representational system), and Section 3 shows you how to examine a person's representational system hierarchy.

By knowing a person's preferred system, you can more easily facilitate the rapport and trust important to effective communication. Knowing a person's representational system hierarchy can help you to understand how people systematically delete certain aspects of experience from their awareness and what those aspects of the environment are most likely to be. With this information, you can help people become alert to situations in which they consistently stop themselves from seeing, feeling oɪ hearing input. As was demonstrated by Sharon in Chapter I (page 11) and the fire victim in Chapter II (page 43), the deletion of portions of experience from a person's model of the world is potentially harmful and limiting to a positive and healthy life.

These mapping techniques can be used at any time during the course of an interview, therapy session or any setting where verbal communication is taking place. The important thing to remember is to maintain continuity and rapport. To suddenly turn to someone and say, "Can you tell me the color of your first car?" may be much less effective than casually, during the course of a conversation, mentioning an anecdote about your first car. Then you can say, "You know, I don't even remember what color it was....Do you remember the color of *your* first car?"

People access all the time. Once you get used to the concept and its uses, you will find that it is usually unnecessary to go through the formal mapping process. Many people will give you all the information you need during the course of a normal conversation.

APPENDIX A

CONSTRAINTS ON OUR
MODELS OF THE WORLD

The diagram which follows illustrates the three constraints which affect the construction of our models of the world. As discussed in Chapter I, we start with the "raw materials" of experience. These are channeled via our sensory organs through our *neurological filters*. At any moment in time, we have available to us one complete 4-Tuple which includes an experience of sight, feeling, sound, taste and smell.

From there, our experience is further modified by language and other *social filters* which either enhance our perception or diminish it.

Finally, our great body of stored memories create an *individual filter* which further modifies our perception, sometimes by heightening and other times by obscuring the original sensory data. This internally generated experience can take the place of any of the four parameters of the 4-T at any moment in time. The completed 4-T with its combination of experiences of external and internal origins is then shuttled into memory, where it may be called upon to modify future experiences as they arise.

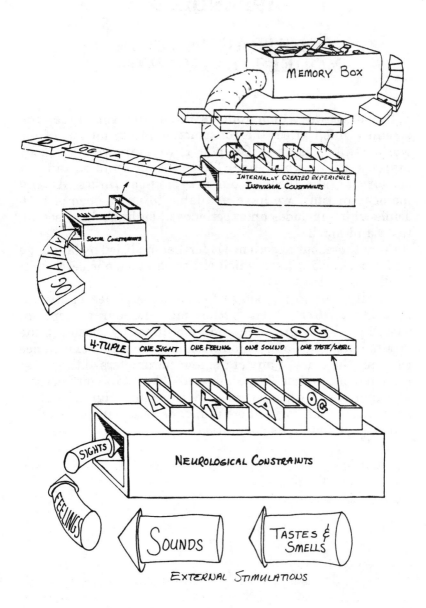

APPENDIX B

THE REPRESENTATIONAL
SYSTEM BIAS TEST

For each of the following statements, place the number 4 next to the phrase that best describes you, a 3 next to the phrase that would next best describe you, and so on, ending with a 1 next to the phrase that least describes you. Do this for each of the five statements. Scoring information follows the test.

1. I make important decisions based on:
   _____ gut level feelings.
   _____ which way sounds the best.
   _____ what looks best to me.
   _____ precise diligent study of the issues.

2. During an argument, I am most likely to be influenced by:
   _____ the other person's tone of voice.
   _____ whether or not I can see the other person's point of view.
   _____ the logic of the other person's argument.
   _____ whether or not I feel I am in touch with the other person's true feelings.

3. I most easily communicate what is going on with me by:
   _____ the way I dress.
   _____ the feelings I share.
   _____ the words I choose.
   _____ my tone of voice.

4. It is easy for me to:
   _____ find the ideal volume and tuning on a stereo system.
   _____ select the most intellectually relevant points concerning an interesting subject.
   _____ select superbly comfortable furniture.
   _____ select rich color combinations.

5. ____ I am very attuned to the sounds in my surroundings.

____ I am very adept at making sense of new facts and data.

____ I am very sensitive to the way articles of clothing feel on my body.

____ I have a strong response to colors and the way a room looks.

Scoring the Representational System Bias Test

Step 1: Copy the answers from the test onto the lines below.

1. ___ K
   ___ A
   ___ V
   ___ D

2. ___ A
   ___ V
   ___ D
   ___ K

3. ___ V
   ___ K
   ___ D
   ___ A

4. ___ A
   ___ D
   ___ K
   ___ V

5. ___ A
   ___ D
   ___ K
   ___ V

Step 2: Add the numbers associated with each letter. There will be five entries for each letter.

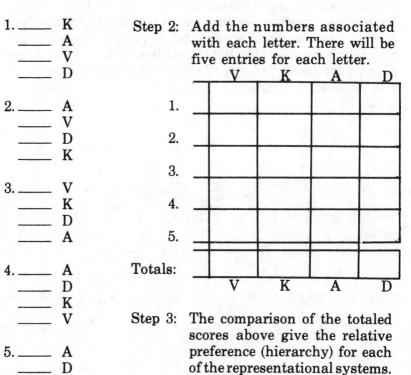

Step 3: The comparison of the totaled scores above give the relative preference (hierarchy) for each of the representational systems.

Note: Obviously, a test as brief as this will not give absolutely accurate data on an individual. However, as a quick and easy tool for identifying potential problems, strengths, and weaknesses between individuals, it has proven quite useful in several settings including analysis of business management styles and in marriage and family counseling sessions. The immediate feedback and the ability to compare scores promotes healthy and productive discussion between participants.

APPENDIX C

THE COMMUNICATION CATEGORIES MODEL

The chart on the following pages is organized around four preferred representational systems. These are the visual system, the kinesthetic system, the auditory system, and the digital system. This chart is an abbreviated visual representation of the model as it is presented in the text. It is a highly generalized format meant to be a guide to *your own observations*. As you grow accustomed to the distinctions presented here, you will also discover and become familiar with the "interpretations" required in its use. Remember, we are all highly complex individuals, and this is only a model of certain communicative behaviors. It is a generalized, deleted, and distorted representation of those behaviors.

Pattern	"Visual"	"Kino"
Predicates which presuppose a representational system	seems, look, bright, perspective, focus, colorful	feel, grasp, touch, firm, warm, cool, get a handle on
Posture	straight, erect, head & shoulders up	curved, bowed, head & shoulders down
Body "type" and movements	either thin or obese; tight, jerky	soft, full, rounded; loose, flowing
Lip size	thin, tight	full, soft
Breathing	high in chest	low, into abdomen
Voice tonality, speed, and volume	high, clear, fast, and loud	low, airy, slow, and soft
Eye elevation in relation to others	above others	below others
Rule for looking while listening	"look to listen"	would rather touch than look
Satir category	"blamer"	"placater"
Meta Model violations	reversed references, modal operators of necessity	unspecified verbs, modal operators of possibility
Meta Model illformed meanings	mind reading	cause and effect
Accessing cues	up left and right	down left or right

"Tonal"	"Digital"	Pattern
tone, loud, rings a bell, sounds like, harmonious	statistically speaking, reasonable, logical, know	Predicates which presuppose a representational system
"telephone" posture, head tilted to side	arms folded, erect, head up	Posture
inconsistent body; between tight & loose	soft, full; rigid	Body "type" and movements
varies	thin, tight	lip size
full range	restricted	breathing
melodic, rhythmic, variable	monotone, clipped, consistent	voice tonality, speed, and volume
often diverted down to listen	"gazes" over others' heads	Eye elevation in relation to others
"don't look to listen"	no eye contact	Rule for looking while listening
"distracter"	"computer"	Satir category
generalized and deleted referential index	generalized and deleted referents, nominalizations	Meta Model violations
lost performative	lost performative	Meta Model illformed meanings
level left and right (head often tilted and down)	level left and right (head often in an up position)	Accessing cues

APPENDIX D

GLOSSARY OF TERMS

The numbers in parentheses following the definitions indicate the page or pages in the text where a more complete explanation of the term may be found.

abstract noun: see "Nominalizations." (84)

accessing cues: movements of the eyes which are symptomatic of cerebral processes of retrieving thoughts and other experiences stored in the brain. (115-122)

analog: any form of output (behavior) exclusive of word-symbols. (69-71)

auditory tape loops: thoughts, expressions, and persistent ideas stored in short, often tuneful or rhythmic auditory patterns.(119)

calibrated communication: sometimes called a "calibrated loop," these are unconscious patterns of communication in which a look, gesture, or expression unintentionally triggers a response from another person. Often based on subliminal cues — minimal gestures that operate outside the awareness of the individuals involved — these calibrated communication loops can be the source of pain-producing miscommunication between couples, family members, and co-workers. (102)

cause and effect: a Meta Model violation in which the speaker indicates a belief that one person can directly cause another person to have a particular emotion. (105-108)

communication categories model: based on the four representational systems, this model includes the behavioral patterns associated with each of the systems (see "represen-

tational systems"). These patterns include predicate preference, posture and body type, breathing, lip size, voice
tonality, eye elevation, rules for looking, Satir categories,
Meta Model violations, Meta Model illformed meanings, and
accessing cues. A complete chart of these behaviors for each
system is included in Appendix C. (48-50)

complex equivalents: the relationship between a word or
action and the *meaning* attached to it by the observer. It is
called "complex," because the equivalent verbal description
is much more detailed than the word or action being defined
("a picture is worth a thousand words"). A person's complex
equivalent is a more accurate representation of his deep
structure associations to the particular word or action. (27-
28)

concrete nouns: see "Nominalizations." (84)

consensus reality: due to similarities in the neurological
mechanisms within each of us and shared social and cultural
experiences we are able to create similar representations of
the world called consensus reality. (4)

constraints: filters on the model-building processes.
Neurological, social, and individual constraints affect our
models of the world by providing experiences to be generalized, deleted, and distorted. (16-27)

deep structure (DS): the most complete linguistic representation of an experience. A person's DS is a linguistic model of
his model of the world. (73)

deletion: the universal human modeling process which
screens out or prevents the awareness of experiences. A
primary function of the brain and central nervous system is
to filter out most sensory input so that we can attend to our
various activities uninterrupted. In language, deletion is the
process of simplifying deep structure representations by
leaving things out in the surface structure. (7)

derived feelings: see "Emotions." (35-36)

distortion: the universal human modeling process by which we manipulate our perceptions and remembered experiences. This process often alters experiences in a way which will better fit our own models of the world, and it is also important in the creative processes of fantasizing, planning ahead, and enjoying works of art and literature. (8)

emotions: a complex set of physical sensations combined with other thought processes such as internal images and thoughts. Emotions are also commonly called "feelings," possibly because of the important role the physical sensations play in our ability to attach meaning to these complex "derived feelings." (35-36)

feedback: see "rapport." (66)

filters: see "constraints." (16)

4-Tuple (4-T): one moment in time including the four parameters of visual, kinesthetic, auditory, and olfactory-gustatory experiences. Written as $\langle V \quad K \quad A \quad O \rangle$. (32)

generalization: the universal human modeling process of drawing from one or one set of experiences to understand and make predictions about similar new experiences. (6)

individual constraints: the collection of our past personal history — our complete set of stored and remembered experiences — through which we filter our ongoing experiences. (23-27)

information retrieval behaviors: movements and gestures which are symptomatic of cerebral processes associated with retrieving stored (remembered) information. These include eye movements (116-122), breathing patterns (122-124), and body posturing (124).

internally generated stimuli: experiences, ⟨V K A O⟩, which are drawn from memory. This "synthetic experience" can include any or all parameters of the 4-T and replaces at the moment in time it is being accessed the associated external experience in the 4-T. (24-26)

lead system: the system a person uses when he first starts to access internally stored information. The lead system is not always the same system as a person's preferred system. (40)

logical typing errors: mistaking the "map" for the "territory" it represents. Assuming that what you perceive (which is based on your own model of the world) is *reality*, and that it is the same as what other people perceive. (15-16)

lost performative: a Meta Model violation in which a person makes a value judgement or expresses a belief in a way that deletes the judge or the originator of the belief. (108-110)

mapping: a process by which you can determine a person's accessing cues schematic, his preferred representational system, and his representational system hierarchy. (125-132)

the Meta Model: a linguistic tool for using portions of a person's spoken or written behavior to determine where he has generalized, deleted, or distorted experiences in his model of the world. It includes specific "Meta Model responses" to these "Meta Model violations" which aid in obtaining a more complete representation from the person's deep structure. Certain responses also help to reconnect the speaker with his deep structure in ways which can expand his perceptions and give him more choices about how to feel and behave. (72-73)

meta perspective: an awareness of the *patterns* involved in the processes of communication as well as the content. (108)

148

mind reading: a Meta Model violation in which a person expresses the idea that it is possible to know what someone else is thinking or feeling with little or no diret feedback. (99-104)

mirroring: see "rapport." (66)

modal operators: Meta Model violations which identify limits to a person's model of the world. Modal operators of necessity (93-94) are exemplified by imperatives such as "should," while modal operators of possibility (94-96) are exemplified by words such as "can't."

model: a representation of a thing or process which is useful as a tool for better understanding what it represents and for predicting how it will operate in various situations. A model is a generalized, deleted, and distorted copy of that which it represents. (1-2)

model of the world: a perceptual representation of our experiences of the world. A personal model of "reality," it differs from person to person depending on their neurological make-up and social and individual experiences. (2, 16)

neurological constraints: the filters of our brain and sensory organs. Differences in people's "sensitivity" to various stimuli accounts in part for differences between people's models of the world. (17-20)

nominalization: a Meta Model violation in which an "abstract noun" is formed by taking a verb (such as "relate") and changing it by the process of linguistic distortion into a noun (like "relationship"). A nominalization differs from a "concrete noun" which names a person, place, or thing. (84-90)

nominalized: dissociated from kinesthetic aspects of experience through the use of language. A "digital" is often described as being "nominalized." (85, 88)

pacing: see "rapport." (66)

occular accessing cues: see "accessing cues." (115-122)

perceptual enhancer: the effects of language on our perception. See also "social constraints." (69)

predicate preference: the habitual use of certain predicates — verbs, adverbs, and adjectives — which indicate systematic use of one of the representational systems to express thoughts more often than the others. Predicate preference is often a good indication of a person's preferred representational system. (37)

preferred representation system: the system in which a person makes the most number of distinctions about himself and his environment. The habitual use of one system more often than the others to sort out and make sense of experiences. (38)

pupil response: an unconscious response to emotional arousal. Directed by the autonomic nervous system, the pupils dilate when a person is exposed to pleasant stimuli and constrict when he is exposed to an unpleasant situation. (113-114)

rapport: during effective communication, rapport is established through communicative behaviors called "pacing." These subtle forms of feedback elicit in the observer a sense of *being like* and of *trusting* the communicator. Two methods of pacing that result in rapport are matching a person's predicate preference and "mirroring" (matching) a person's posture, gestures, rate of breathing, etc. (13-16, 66)

referential index: a Meta Model violation in which the person or thing doing or receiving the action of the verb in a sentence has been deleted (77-78), unspecified (78-80), generalized (80-81), or reversed (82-83).

150

representational systems: literally referring to representations of experience (32), they include the visual system (39, 51-52), the kinesthetic system (39, 52-53), the auditory system (40, 54-55), the digital system (33, 55-56), and the olfactory system (36-37).

representational system hierarchy: the order of responsiveness to the world with the system in which a person makes the most number of distinctions (his preferred representational system) coming first and the least number of distinctions coming last. (47-48)

Satir categories: exaggerated postures and associated internal feelings about oneself. These include the "blamer," "placater," "computer," and "distracter." (62-64)

social constraints: cultural filters on our ability to perceive. Language, for example, can either enhance our perception of something by naming it ("perceptual enhancer"), or it can limit perception by not providing labels for certain aspects of experience. (20-23)

stress: an important factor in determining how a person will respond in certain situations. Stress will often cause a person to "retreat" into the representational system in which he makes the most number of distinctions (his preferred system), thereby limiting both his awareness of the world and his choices about how to respond. (42-43)

subliminal cues: see "calibrated communication." (102)

surface structure (SS): the spoken or written portion of communication which is derived from the DS using the processes of generalization, deletion, and distortion. (73)

synthetic experience: see "internally generated stimuli." (24-26)

trust: within the context of effective communication, trust is the sense a person gets when he believes he is being understood. Trust is a necessary ingredient in the "magic" of effective communication and change. (13-16)

universal human modeling processes: three mechanisms common to all model-building activities; the processes of generalization, deletion, and distortion. (5-9)

universal quantifier: a Meta Model violation in which a generalization has been made in a way that indicates that the speaker is not aware of any exceptions to his statement as with such words as "every" and "never." (96-99)

unspecified verbs: a Meta Model violation in which a person uses a verb which deletes such qualities as how, when, or where the activity took place or the duration or intensity of the act. (90-92)

8

152

FOOTNOTES

Footnotes for Chapter I

1. For the purpose of this work, the distinction between
"ourselves" and our surrounding environment is a functional one. It does not imply that other ways of describing the
relationship do not exist. As Jung points out in *Psychological Types,* psychology focuses on internal processes which
operate inside both the subject and the observer. Therefore,
"...the observer should be...able to see not only subjectively
but also objectively. The demand that he should see *only*
objectively is quite out of the question, for it is impossible. We
must be satisfied if he does not see *too* subjectively." (p. 9)
Roger N. Walsh also makes a contribution to the discussion
in the following quote from the *Journal of Transpersonal
Psychology:*

> What can be known is the interaction between
> the observer and the observed and never the
> independent properties of the observed alone.
> All observation is a function of the observer,
> and thus the known universe is inextricably
> linked with consciousness.... (p. 180)

2. *Volume I* of *The Structure of Magic* contains many of the
models presented in this work. The "universal human
modeling processes" are presented on pages 14 — 18. I highly
recommend any of Bandler and Grinder's books (see the
Bibliography at the end of this book).

3. This is a linguistic form called a "nominalization." See
Chapter III for a complete discussion of this and other
linguistic indications of the structure of a person's model of
the world.

4. From Coleman and Foresman, *Abnormal Psychology
and Modern Life,* 1972.

5. The study was printed under the title *Patients View
Their Psychotherapy* in 1969.

6. From *Steps to an Ecology of Mind,* 1972. See his discussion on the "theory of logical types" which begins on page 280.

7. *The Structure of Magic, Vol. I,* pages 8 — 13, give Bandler and Grinder's rendition. Watzlawick, et al, gives the definition of *constraint* in *Pragmatics of Human Communication* as follows:

> According to information theory, stochastic processes show *redundancy* or *constraint,* two terms which can be used interchangeably with the concept of *pattern....* (p.34)

As used in this book, then, constraints are patterns which operate on the model-building processes. They can be conceptualized as a "grid" or "filter" through which information is processed on the way to becoming an experience.

8. See pages 4 and 174 of *The Structure of Magic,* Vol. II, by Bandler and Grinder, 1976.

9. Whorf's "linguistic-relativity hypotheses" is a well-formed presentation of the idea that thought is relative to the language in which it is constructed. In *Language, Thought, and Reality,* he proposes that it is the structure of language which causes culturally seated differences in perception.

10. Bandler and Grinder, *Frogs into Princes,* 1979, p. 15.

11. Coleman and Foresman, *Abnormal Psychology and Modern Life,* 1972.

12. This is somewhat different from the eye-contact rule discussed in association with the visual communication category in Chapter II. However, it is not unusual for conflict to occur as a result of an encounter between someone operating with the social eye-contact model and someone else operating out of the visual system.

13. See *The Structure of Magic, Vol I,* page 19, footnote 2.

14. From Bandler, Grinder, and Satir, *Changing with Families,* 1976, comes the following definitions:

> *Complex Equivalence* is the relationship between a word or set of words and some experience which those words name. (p.90)

Footnotes for Chapter II

1. The term *representational system* comes from Bandler and Grinder. For additional information, see *The Structure of Magic, Vol. I,* pages 6-26.
2. In keeping with the Bandler-Grinder model, I have put the olfactory and gustatory systems together. The name "olfactory" and symbol "0" are used because we make so many more distinctions with our sense of smell than with our sense of taste, which can only differentiate between four basic stimuli: sweet, sour, salty, and bitter.
3. From *Pragmatics of Human Communication,* page 63.
4. Bandler and Grinder discuss "the most highly valued representational system" on page 8 of *The Structure of Magic, Vol. II.* They also expand on page 26, saying, "By most highly valued representational system we mean the ... system the person typically uses to bring information into consciousness...," and "...no special one of the... systems is better than the others, although some may be more efficient for certain tasks." I have incorporated this construct into "preferred representational system" in its greatly expanded form presented in this book.
5. From *Visual Learning, Thinking and Communication.*
6. Unlike information entering our brains from the other sensory systems, smell does not pass through the thalamus and is, therefore, not subjected to the thalamic filtering the other systems undergo.
7. See the section "Trust: Gaining Rapport" in Chapter I.
8. For more information, see the section "Mapping" in Chapter IV.
9. Especially important is her book *Peoplemaking* which will be referred to later in this section.
10. The two books, *The Structure of Magic, Volumes I* and *II,* already referred to contain part of the information used to create the communication categories model presented in this book.
11. This chart was developed primarily through the work of Frank Pucelik of the M.E.T.A. Institute with input from students in various parts of the United States. It would be

interesting to compare these observations with those of individuals from other cultural backgrounds.

12. From Coleman and Foresman, *Abnormal Psychology and Modern Life,* page 642.

13. Wiliam Sheldon, author of *The Varieties of Human Physique* and *The Varieties of Human Temperament,* is famous for his research on the relationship between temperament and physique. Although this book presents correlations between various patterns of behavior including body types, the need for further research poses exciting possibilities to experimental psychologists and others in the field of human communications.

14. From an interview with Edward T. Hall in the August, 1979, *Psychology Today.*

15. See the section *Constraints on the Model* in Chapter I, especially "Social Constraints."

16. This is another example of a complex equivalent (see pages 27-28 in Chapter I). In this case, a particular meaning, "lying," is attached to a specific behavior, looking away while talking. Thus, a behavior which is necessary to the person who needs to look away while talking can pose problems if it is misinterpreted by someone with the above complex equivalent. There is an excellent discussion of complex equivalents in Bandler, Grinder, and Satir's *Changing with Families,* which begins on page 38.

17. See pages 59-85 in *Peoplemaking* by Virginia Satir for a complete presentation of her "patterns of communication."

18. See *The Structure of Magic, Vol. II,* page 47.

Footnotes for Chapter III

1. As Gregory Bateson says on page 291 in *Steps to an Ecology of Mind,* "It would seem that analogic communication is in some sense more primitive than digital and that there is a broad evolutionary trend toward the substitution of digital for analogic mechanisms in higher mammals."

2. Bateson does point out *context markers* which may signal one interpretation as being correct. See pages 289 — 291 in *Steps to an Ecology of Mind.*

3. See *The Structure of Magic, Vol. I.* The form I present here is a revision of their original model. This version deletes some of the original distinctions and expands other distinctions. I highly recommend reading the original version for more information on the origins and development of the Meta Model.

4. Because of differences in the structure of different languages, some of the distinctions presented here may not apply to the native speakers of languages other than English.

5. From Noam Chomsky's *Language and Mind* comes, "...we can thus distinguish the *surface structure* of the sentence, the organization into categories and phrases that is directly associated with the physical signal, from the underlying *deep structure,* also a system of categories and phrases, but with a more abstract character." (p. 28—29) These two are related, says Chomsky, by certain formal operations known as *grammatical transformations* which include the processes of generalization, deletion, and distortion.

6 From *Omni Magazine,* November, 1978.

7. For an elegant and pragmatic discussion of the calibrated communication cycle in families, see Bandler, Grinder and Satir, *Changing with Families,* especially Part II.

Footnotes for Chapter IV

1. From "Learning the Arabs' Silent Language," an interview with Edward T. Hall, *Psychology Today,* August, 1979, pages 47-48.

2. See his chapter "Pupil Signals," which begins on page 169. This book is an excellent and stimulating resource for anyone interested in human behavior.

3. See Hess' book *The Tell-tale Eye* for a complete description of this phenomenon.

4. See their book *Frogs into Princes,* pages 22-27.

5. For more information, see Sperry's article in *Handbook of Clinical Neurology.*

6. From Bogen: "Some Educational Aspects of Hemispheric Specialization" in Betty Edwards *Drawing on the Right Side of the Brain.*

7. For a fascinating discussion on the nature of internal dialog, see Donald Meichenbaum's book *Cognitive Behavior Modification.*

8. Notice the therapist's intentional use of the cause and effect pattern here. In this way he paces Joe's experience and uses the pattern to ensure good rapport. This utilization of a Meta Model violation is an effective out-of-awareness means of operating within the client's model of the world in a way which enhances the trust important to therapeutic communication. Asking this way also elicits an uninhibited demonstration of the dysfunctional pattern that is preventing the client from being able to change. The observant therapist can utilize this piece of the client's model of the world in very productive ways as the session continues.

BIBLIOGRAPHY

Bandler, R. and Grinder, J. *Frogs into Princes.* Moab, Utah: Real People Press, 1979.

_____. *The Structure of Magic, Vol. I.* Palo Alto, California: Science and Behavior Books, 1975.

_____. *The Structure of Magic, Vol. II.* Palo Alto, California: Science and Behavior Books, 1976.

Bandler, R., Grinder, J., and Satir, V. *Changing with Families.* Palo Alto, California; Science and Behavior Books, 1976.

Bateson, G. *Steps to an Ecology of Mind.* New York: Ballantine Books, 1972.

Bogen, J. "Some Educational Aspects of Hemispheric Specialization." *U.C.L.A. Educator*, 17 (1975): 24-32.

Bois, J. S. *The Art of Awareness, Third Ed.* Dubuque, Iowa: W. C. Brown Co., 1966.

Castaneda, C. *Tales of Power.* New York: Simon and Shuster, 1974.

Coleman, J. C. and Foresman, S. *Abnormal Psychology and Modern Life, Fourth Ed.* Glenview, Illinois: Scott, Foresman and Company, 1972.

Chomsky, N. *Language and Mind: Enlarged Ed.* New York: Harcourt, Brace, Jovanovich, Inc., 1972.

Edwards, B. *Drawing on the Right Side of the Brain.* New York: St. Martin's Press, 1979.

Ellerbroek, W. "Language, Emotion and Disease." *Omni*, 1:2, Nov., 1978, 93-120.

Frank, J. D. *Persuasion and Healing.* Baltimore: Johns Hopkins University Press, 1973.

Gibran, K. *The Prophet.* New York: Alfred A. Knopf, 1969.

Hall, E. T. *Beyond Culture.* New York: Anchor Press/ Doubleday and Co., 1976.

———. "Learning the Arab's Silent Language." *Psychology Today,* 13:3, Aug., 1979, 45-54.

———. *The Silent Language.* New York: Doubleday and Co., 1959.

Hess, E. *The Tell-tale Eye.* New York, 1975.

Huxley, A. *The Doors of Perception.* New York: Harper and Row, 1954.

Jung, C. G. *Man and His Symbols.* Garden City, New York: Doubleday, 1964.

———. *Psychological Types* (Vol VI of the Collected Works. Princeton: Princeton University Press, 1971 (1923).

Meichenbaum, D. *Cognitive Behavior Modification.* New York: Prenum Press, 1977.

Morris, D. *Manwatching.* New York: Harry N. Abrams, Inc., 1977.

Palazzoli, M., Gianfranco, C., Giuiana, P. and Luigi, B. *Paradox and Counterparadox.* New York: Jason Aronson, 1978.

Samuels, M. and Samuels, N. *Seeing with the Mind's Eye.* New York: Random House, 1975.

Satir, V. *Peoplemaking*. Palo Alto, California: Science and Behavior Books, 1972.

Sheldon, W. H. *The Varieties of Human Physique*. New York: Harper and Brothers, 1940.

Shepard, M. *Fritz*. New York: Bantam Books, Inc., 1975.

Shepard, R. *Visual Learning, Thinking and Communication*, edited by B. S. Randhawa and W. E. Coffman. New York: Academic Press, 1978.

Sperry, R. W., M. S. Gazzaniga, and J. E. Bogen, "Interhemispheric Relationships: the Neocortical Commissures; Syndromes of Hemisphere Disconnection," *Handbook of Clinical Neurology*, P. J. Vinken and G. W. Bruyn, eds., Amsterdam: North-Holland Publishing Co., 1969, 273-289.

Strupp, H. H., Fox, R. E., and Lessler, K. *Patients View Their Psychotherapy*. Baltimore: Johns Hopkins University Press, 1969.

Walsh, R. Emerging cross-disciplinary parallels: Suggestions from the neurosciences. *Journal of Transpersonal Psychology*, 11:2, 175-184, 1979.

Watzlawick, P., Beavin, J. and Jackson, D. *Pragmatics of Human Communication*. New York: W. W. Norton and Co., 1967.

Whorf, B. L. In Carol, J. B. (ed.) *Language, Thought, and Reality*. New York: Wiley, 1956.

About The Authors

Byron A. Lewis, M.A., is the director of the Meta Training Institute, a Northwest Educational and Consulting firm specializing in the techniques of Neuro-Linguistic Programming. As an undergraduate student at UCSC in the mid-1970s, Byron studied under Dr. John Grinder and participated in the original research which laid the foundation for the now popular field of NLP.

Even before receiving his Masters in Psychology, Byron was actively involved in teaching communications seminars. A personable and entertaining seminar leader and consultant, Byron has been conducting seminars and workshops in the field of Neuro-Linguistic Programming since 1977.

R. Frank Pucelik, Ph.D. is widely recognized as one of the world's finest trainers in interpersonal communication and success strategies for change. His zest and profound skills also make him one of the most entertaining presenters in the field of Meta communication today.

Currently the President of META International, Inc., a behavioral sciences consulting firm, Frank has been leading seminars and workshops since the early 1970's. An original member of the Bandler and Grinder research team, Frank's impressive range of knowledge comes from his extensive training in a variety of communication techniques and their scientific basis.

METAMORPHOUS PRESS

Metamorphous Press is a publisher of books and other media providing resources for personal growth and positive change. MP publishes leading-edge ideas that help people strengthen their unique talents and discover that we are responsible for our own realities. Many of our titles center around Neurolinguistic Programming (NLP). NLP is an exciting, practical, and powerful model of observable patterns of behavior and communication and the processes that underlie them.

Metamorphous Press provides selections in many useful subject areas such as communication, health and fitness, education, business and sales, therapy, selections for young persons, and other subjects of general and specific interest. Our products are available in fine bookstores around the world.

Our distributors for North America are:

Baker & Taylor   Moving Books, Inc.
Bookpeople   New Leaf
Inland Book Co.   Pacific Pipeline
Metamorphous   The Distributors
  Advanced Product Services

For those of you overseas, we are distributed by:

Airlift (UK, Western Europe)
Specialist Publications (Australia)

New selections are added regularly and availability and prices change, so ask for a current catalog or to be put on our mailing list. If you have difficulty finding our products in your favorite store, or if you prefer to order by mail, we will be happy to make our books and other products available to you directly. Your involvement and interest in what we do is always welcome. Please write or call us at:

Metamorphous Press
P.O. Box 10616
Portland, OR 97210
(503) 228-4972

TOLL FREE ORDERING
1-800-937-7771

SKILL BUILDER SERIES

The **SKILL BUILDER SERIES** is a series of technique-building books covering all abilities from the beginner in NLP to the trainer. These manuals and workbooks will help you integrate and extend your knowledge gained through seminars or other books on NLP.

The Excellence Principle by Scout Lee, Ed.D. is a beginning manual filled with everything you need to get started with NLP. It was developed from Dr. Lee's notes written to present this exciting technology to the academic community. Filled with pictures, charts and diagrams to illustrate the concepts, this book will teach the reader skills in an amazing technology.
ISBN: 1-55552-003-0 Pbk.

Basic Techniques, Book I is a workbook designed for those who want to master the skills of NLP and for whom training is unavailable or not enough. This guidebook includes a set of practical, easy exercises you can do by yourself to integrate NLP skills you may learn in other books or seminars.
ISBN: 1-55552-016-2 Pbk.

Basic Techniques, Book II contains exercises a step further than Book I. Written for the reader who understands the essentials of NLP, this guidebook reinforces existing knowledge, provides clarification of terms, and gives step-by-step instructional exercises which can be done with two or more individuals. It is a valuable resource for those wishing to extend their skills in study groups.
ISBN: 1-55552-005-7 Pbk.

Your Balancing Act: Discovering New Life Through Five Dimensions of Wellness is the first of several planned workbooks of applied NLP technology, applied here to belief change in health and wellness. This workbook helps you to balance physical, emotional, social, mental and spiritual belief systems for optimum wellness.
ISBN: 0-943920-75-2 Pbk.

Advanced Techniques is designed as a reference for trainers. It is a collection of exercises of varying complexity detailed in the form of lesson plans. Information is provided with the intention of helping the leader of a group to assist the participants in getting maximum benefit from the exercises.
ISBN: 0-943920-08-6 Pbk.

The Challenge of Excellence applies NLP technology to leadership training. The "Challenge of Excellence" is an outdoor course of physical and emotional challenges on ropes, balance beams and poles where people test their limits and abilities--metaphors for the challenges of everyday life. Using NLP, this book shows the mind/body interconnection and our capacity for learning patterns of excellence.
ISBN: 1-55552-004-9 Pbk.

Get The Results You Want

Kim Kostere & Linda Malatesta
This book offers the knowledge and NLP skills necessary to make the process of personal change exciting and rewarding. It provides all people who work in innerpersonal communication and changework with a sound, step-by-step process for more effective results.
1-55552-015-4 Pbk.

POSITIVE CHANGE GUIDES

Magic of NLP Demystified

Byron Lewis & Frank Pucelik
This introductory NLP book gives readers a clear and understandable overview of the subject. It covers the basic concepts of NLP using "user-friendly" illustrations and graphics. One of the best introductory books available for new NLP students.
1-55552-017-0 Pbk.
0-943920-09-4 Cloth

Fitness Without Stress

Robert M. Rickover
This book explains the Alexander Technique, recognized today to be one of the most powerful methods of improving body movement and coordination as well as overall health. It is also a guide to finding an Alexander teacher. No previous experience necessary.
0-943920-32-9 Cloth

The Power of Balance

Brian W. Fahey, Ph.D.
The importance of balance in life is the emphasis of Fahey's book. It expands on the original ideas about balancing body structure, known as "Rolfing." Reading this thought-provoking text can be a step toward achieving high levels of energy and well-being.
0-943920-52-3 Cloth

These are only a few of the titles we offer. If you cannot find our books at your local bookstore, you can order directly from us. Call or write for our free catalog:

Metamorphous Press
P.O. Box 10616
Portland, OR 97210
(503) 228-4972

Toll Free Ordering 1-800-937-7771
FAX 503-223-9117

Shipping and handling charges are $3.75 for each book and $1.00 for each additional title. (Foreign orders include $4.00 for each book and $2.00 for each additional title). We ship UPS unless otherwise requested. All orders must be prepaid in U.S. dollars. Call toll free to determine additional charges, to use a credit card, or to request a catalog. Prices and availability subject to change without notice.